What Cooks at Stillmeadow

What Cooks
at Stillmeadow

THE FAVORITE RECIPES OF

Gladys Taber

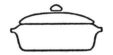

J. B. LIPPINCOTT COMPANY
PHILADELPHIA AND NEW YORK

To

ALICE BLINN

In memory of so many happy hours

Books by Gladys Taber

Contents

What Cooks at Stillmeadow

Foreword

MY BATTLE WITH COOKING began when, as a bride, I was suddenly faced with the job of getting three meals a day. My Camp-Fire repertoire of Shrimp Wiggle and fudge was hardly a basis for all-round home-cooking. It was then I learned that being able to play the mandolin, fix bouquets, and recite "Alas, poor Yorick, I knew him well," did not add up to the main thing in living. Man may not live by bread alone, but he certainly cannot live without it.

I was fortified for my bout with the art of cooking by two good cookbooks, a blue organdy apron, some embroidered dish towels (East, West, Home's Best), some shiny utensils (all the wrong sizes), a Hoosier cabinet, and a leaky gas stove. Humming "Margie," I leafed through the cookbooks. All the recipes sounded wonderful. But since I did not know what Braise meant, I was in trouble right away. Sauté defeated me entirely. And Dredge with Flour had me licked. Since my father was a geologist, I knew all about dredging silt up from river bottoms and finding fossils. But to dredge with flour?

For me, in those days, eggs did not separate, they ran together. Pastry never fitted the pie tin and when I tried to piece it out, the pieces came off in the oven.

11

Cookies glued themselves irrevocably to the cookie sheet. Cakes sank in the middle like a Grand Canyon. Those tender juicy roasts withered away in the oven, and my steaks needed buzz saws served alongside.

We survived this period of disaster chiefly because my mother came over every afternoon with a basket covered with a clean linen napkin. Crisp fried chicken, fresh peas cooked with a mint leaf, a wedge of juicy deep-dish apple pie, still warm. She just happened to have made extra, she always said.

She was worried because I had never had time to learn to cook. I was always going to school and so busy. She didn't want to interfere with my career. But as I threw another pie in the garbage, I wished I knew less Mediaeval History and a little more about food.

When we moved to a town halfway across the country I had to buckle down in earnest. I studied my cookbooks day and night. I practised. And, like every beginning cook, I found I could learn to make separate dishes but that I could never get everything done at the same time. We ate a number of meals with buttered carrots (slightly burned) as a first course, followed some time later by the meat, when it got done, and much, much later by the baked potatoes which seemed to sit endlessly in the oven and stay like cement. I seldom had time for salad, because I was too busy trying to get the main meal done.

Then, too, I had trouble with the cookbooks themselves. As I studied the recipes, I discovered the fateful word MEANWHILE. I was supposed to separate eggs, then beat them, MEANWHILE stirring something constantly. I was to melt butter, blend in flour and gradually add milk, MEANWHILE dicing or peeling something, and not forgetting to test that cake in the oven with a clean broomstraw. MEANWHILE I was theoretically tossing the salad. And so, when I finally got a semblance of a meal scrambled onto the table, I was too nervous to eat.

The most important lesson I learned was not to get in a panic when I saw MEANWHILE staring at me. As I raised a buttered finger to turn the page I let the mean-whiles shift for themselves. A good many of them could, and did, wait until I got to them! The minute I came to this decision, I began to relax and cooking got easier.

As time went on, to my utmost astonishment, people who came to dinner asked to have certain dishes again! I began to jot down on stray bits of paper the ones I used most often and were favorites. I collected recipes with the same fervor stamp collectors go after special stamps. However, since I had absolutely no system, many of the choice ones would get lost. I had a drawerful, and two shelves in the kitchen cupboard stuffed with more. I also had recipes written on all the blank pages in my cookbooks. I got more cookbooks, until I finally possessed thirty-six. I discovered what a pleasure cookbooks can be, just to browse through. Nobody, I felt, could live long enough to try all the recipes in the books, but what fun to sit by the apple-wood fire at night and read about exotic dishes. I liked them all, from How To Cook a Bear's Paw, to what to do with Langusta. Recipes can carry one from hot tropical islands to cosy Swedish kitchens.

I sometimes lay it to the pineapple upside-down cake, that I began to think of filing my favorites. This particular recipe was given me when I was married, and by the time I could cook, it was a special favorite. It was lost for two years, during which time I tried dozens of upside-down cakes. The family opined they were all good, but not like the missing one. It turned up in a small battered envelope labeled salads. I went out and bought a file.

From this time on, I dug up people's favorite specialties as a truffle hound digs for truffles. I ran up against a few misguided friends who kept their best dishes a SECRET. But most women love to share the good things of life. "Please tell me how you make this," usually brings a copy of the recipe, even if it has been a family recipe for seventy-five years.

The recipes in this particular book are personal favorites, chosen from all the recipes I know because they are the ones we have liked best at Stillmeadow. Many of them have memories, such as Poor Man's Stew, which we cooked over the fireplace during a hurricane. Belle's Wednesday Salad was a gift from a dear friend who had no money to buy presents with, but shared her best recipe, giving her love with it. A few were invented during blizzards when we were snowbound and guests were snowed in with us. Hurricane Duck evolved when we piled bath towels against window ledges and piled a sack of potatoes against the back door to keep it shut. We could not get to the woodpile, so the fireplace cooking was out, but we had a charcoal grill and a small bag of charcoal. And some left-over duck which would spoil with no current on in the refrigerator.

While trees crashed outside and wind and rain roared from a black sky, we lit candles, and burned an orange crate in the fireplace and stirred the hurricane duck over the glowing charcoal. No meal ever tasted better!

Stillmeadow favorites have to pass two tests, aside from tasting good. They must be easy to make, as far as preparation time goes. The elaborate ones that take hours, such as many of the elegant French dishes, are for reading about, but not for me to cook. As with most women in our day, my kitchen time is budgeted. Most of us nowadays either cook with the babies bucketing around underfoot or cook after a hard day's work in an office when the urge to get the feet up and rest is almost overpowering.

Occasionally, on a weekend, with a baby sitter or a willing husband, the gourmet cook can give herself up to a day getting one fabulous meal together, but since I never had a baby sitter, and since there were always about twenty hours of work to do before I could think of dinner, I never personally added the gourmet recipes to my favorites. The gourmet recipes I read in bed.

Secondly, my real favorites are recipes that call for ingredients that are readily available. Having lived for twenty-five years on my forty-acre farm in a rather isolated part of New England, I cook according to what can be had. Happy the day when our village grocery laid in a stock of herbs. I tried growing my own and drying them, but it was not exactly a howling success. Mint, borage, chives, sage, dill, did well, but tarragon died out the first winter. Now I buy my herbs at the market, and am thankful.

My adventures in cooking have involved a good many kinds of heat. I have cooked over a single kerosene heater, over a campfire, over a fireplace fire, over a leaky gas stove in the city, over a wood-burning iron cookstove, and over a modern electric range with all kinds of push buttons. I believe you can cook well with almost any kind of heat, provided you understand its limitations. An old-fashioned wood stove turns out the most delectable meals, but you do have to be very intelligent about when to feed in more wood. A quick heady gas stove is a wonder. An electric range is steady and reliable and if you can work the automatic timers, which I cannot do, you may put your dinner in before you go to the Woman's Club and still keep your husband happy, because dinner will be ready on time. But I used to make very good pies and biscuits over that little kerosene stove.

Because of the variation of cooking units, every woman must know her own. Modern ranges should have the ovens calibrated, and seldom do. Gas and electric pressures may vary, and what is 350° for one oven may turn out to be 425° by another. Therefore, I feel the old-fashioned test with a straw or a knife inserted in the center or bubbling and turning golden is best.

I have a horrid memory of baking potatoes for six hours in my oven. The thermostat had gone off.

With pressure cookers, deep freezers, electric skillets and all the marvelous household aids now available we have come a long way from the early days. We also have canned and frozen foods, packaged foods ready to cook, new seasonings, spices, even whole meals ready to heat up and serve. But so far as I know, no one has invented a packaged cook! Cooking still needs an individual touch, a bit of imagination, and a hand with ingredients.

The reason cooking is such fun is that there is always a discovery just around the corner. You never can sit down and say, I know it all. Women who claim to be bored with cooking, I think, have not realized how much of gracious living goes along with a candle-lit table and a bubbling casserole or a chicken basted with a good

16

sauce. Good conversation flourishes over a savory dinner, tension eases, and fatigue gives way to just plain enjoyment. In this curious time we live in, often the family gathers only at the dinner table. But a good meal, shared in leisurely fashion, can be the focal point of the family as a unit.

The recipes I have included in this book are the special favorites at Stillmeadow. Some of them have appeared from time to time in the Diary of Domesticity in *The Ladies' Home Journal,* some of them in articles on cooking, and in my various country books. Some of them have been exchanged with neighbors leaning over the picket fence when the rambler roses are in bloom. Some are traditional family recipes, and some, of course, came out of my own head. Now and then, eating out in a fancy restaurant, I have retired completely from the conversation while I figured out just what made that particular dish so good. Often I have gone home and tried it the next day, with some success. Sometimes I would go back again and again, and never get that one herb pinned down, only to find the recipe in the home-town newspaper a year or so later next to advice to Gloria not to keep telephoning that man who stopped taking her out on dates.

Since we do all of our own cooking and serving and dish-washing at Stillmeadow, my favorites tend to be easily dished up and not to require many pans at once. And most of them are of the sort that will keep while some guest who has lost the way drives to New Haven and back three times before finding Jeremy Swamp Road.

A word about being a hostess. I avidly read all the articles about saving time for a hot perfumed bath, a twenty-minute lie-down, and slipping into a fresh frock, greeting the guests smelling of your best White Lilac and with a rosebud pinned in your hair. Gracious and relaxed. This, however, does not happen to me. Even if an official from the Hague is coming, all the dogs and cats have to be fed on time. The man to repair the washing machine comes around six o'clock (and we bless him for working after hours). The neighbor's cows get in the garden and we may be chasing heifers away from the sweet corn just as company comes. Or, if it is winter, we have to get the cable hooked up to the car and help haul somebody out of the ditch. Or someone phones to say, "Have you seen my Siamese cats? They are gone!" Naturally we have to hunt Siamese cats at that point.

Perhaps the most frequent preliminary to a company dinner at Stillmeadow is the ringing of the phone, and the subsequent announcement: "Turn everything off. The Carringtons' car has broken down and she is about to have her baby, and her husband is at work and we have to get her to the hospital." Or "Jennie has a blacksnake in the cellar, get the rake and come on. She is terrified."

This is part of being a good neighbor. And when our barn burned down, half the village simply left everything, bundled the children up in the back seats of the cars, and came to spend most of the night helping.

Everything we ate for days tasted of burned barn, but the memory of the good neighbors made every bite ambrosial. Almost anything is good, seasoned with love and friendship.

Herewith, the special favorites from Stillmeadow kitchen which I think are favorites worth sharing with my neighbors wherever they live.

Appetizers

WHEN I WAS GROWING UP, company for dinner arrived when invited. If my mother asked guests for 6:30, at 6:30 the last hat, the last coat, the last bead bag were put away, and the candles were already leaking wax on the damask tablecloth. We never sat around sipping and nibbling for an hour or so. Hard liquor was reserved in the medicine cabinet for adding to hot lemonade (1 teaspoon to a lemon) for grippe. Soft drinks were rare, and enjoyed at Fourth of July picnics. Tomato juice had yet to blush over the horizon. Coffee, tea, milk, hot chocolate, lemonade and raspberry shrub were the liquids we consumed.

Tea was served in the afternoon with cucumber sandwiches (in season), tiny cakes and mints. Or sometimes thimble-sized hot biscuits with fresh currant jelly.

But in those days people dropped in just casually, to visit. Even the men, with an hour off from college classes or from selling a nice gingerbread house, would drop in and drink strong tea and eat cress sandwiches.

Entertaining has changed. The coffeeklatsch has come in for young marrieds. Cocktail parties are common. And when company comes for dinner the hostess must count on a considerable lapse of time before everybody gets there. The rise of the appetizer has helped to make waiting for those late-comers easy. A tray of snacks laid before the open fire in winter or on the terrace in summer is inviting and makes for relaxation. The drinks to go with them can suit anybody's taste. Chilled tomato juice, spiked with Worcestershire sauce and garnished with lemon makes a fine pre-dinner drink. Cranberry juice with a lime slice adds color and zest. Clam juice has come lately into favor (sprinkle with freshly ground pepper). Clam and tomato juice mixed are delicious.

If dinner is not to be too heavy, bouillon on the rocks is a good prelude. (Pour canned bouillon over ice cubes, garnish with parsley diced fine, and serve in chilled six-ounce glasses.)

For those who wish cocktails or highballs, these can be served on a separate tray, but it is well to let everyone mix his own. By the time the hostess has sorted out who wants plain water with bourbon, who wants ice but no water, who wants soda but no ice and a little Scotch, and who wants half a jigger of rye in a glass of gingerale, she will have forgotten the roast entirely.

For a party, I favor one hot appetizer and one or two cold ones. I have found that I could spend half a day making dips and spreads and canapés and the guests would invariably settle for the hot clam and cheese dip and the cool smooth cucumber dunk. Or they will clean up Barbara's Hot Canapés and a whole Caviar Island and leave the rest. In other words, if they like one appetizer, they keep right on eating that one. And nothing is deader than a tray of fancy appetizers left over. You cannot make anything out of them. Even my cockers and Irish setter merely lick off the fish paste and let the pimento stars go.

There are any number of crispy crunchy tidbits you can buy and simply turn into that wedding silver bowl. And for dunking, there are more kinds of crackers and chips than I can count. Most of them are improved by heating in a warm oven, and some of them take kindly to a sprinkle of seasoned salt, Parmesan cheese, or garlic powder.

Herewith my special favorites for the appetizer tray, easy to do and easy to eat. They should be served with whatever drinks you choose, but served especially with neighborly talk and a warm welcome.

BARBARA'S HOT CANAPÉS

Cut slices of bread with a doughnut or cookie cutter into rounds. Use firm bread, day old, that will not crumble.

Mix deviled ham (a small or large can according to how many people you are serving) with horseradish to taste. (Use freshly ground horseradish if you have a garden.)

Taste as you mix.

Butter the bread rounds lightly and spread with the mix. Sprinkle a few capers on top of each canapé. Bake in a hot (oven 400°) until bubbly.

Serve hot.

N.B. Save the crusts to toast and crumble for toppings on casseroles or creamed dishes. No waste. We find men like these canapés especially, so make enough if you have men to feed—and what is more fun than feeding men?

AVOCADO DIP

1 cup mashed avocado pulp
½-pound package Philadelphia cream cheese
3 tablespoons lemon juice
⅓ cup minced onions or shallots
1 teaspoon salt
Worcestershire sauce to taste

Blend avocado and cheese well. Add remaining ingredients and mix well. Serve in a bowl with crisp crackers arranged around it.

CHEESE CUBES

3 thick slices bread, white (preferably unsliced until you slice)
2 tablespoons melted butter or margarine
1 egg, beaten
1 cup grated American cheese

Cut the bread into 1-inch cubes. Add egg to butter or margarine and dip the cubes in this mixture, then roll in the cheese. Bake in a moderate oven (350°) until cheese is melted and cubes are golden brown. Serve hot.

BARBECUED BEEF BOWL

1½ pounds hamburger (or 4 cups diced cooked beef)
1½ cups water
¼ cup vinegar
¼ cup sugar
5 teaspoons prepared mustard
Salt, pepper, Cayenne to taste
3 thin lemon slices
2 medium onions, diced
½ cup butter or margarine
1 cup catsup
4 tablespoons Worcestershire sauce

Sauté the onions in the butter or margarine until golden in a deep heavy pan. Add water, vinegar, sugar, mustard, seasonings, and lemons and simmer 20 minutes. Meanwhile brown the hamburger. Add hamburger, catsup and Worcestershire and simmer about 30 minutes. Serve with toast rounds for dunking, and be sure the guests have plates.

N.B. If you use left-over already cooked meat, do not sauté it. This is good for a party that will run latish, because the barbecue is hearty fare.

BLENDER PARTY DIP

1 No. 2½ can pork and beans or chili (without meat)
½ cup shredded Cheddar cheese
½ clove garlic, minced
½ teaspoon salt
1 teaspoon chili powder (omit this if you use canned chili)
Dash Tabasco
2 teaspoons vinegar
2 teaspoons Worcestershire
4 slices bacon, broiled and broken in bits

Combine all ingredients, except the bacon, in the blender, and blend on medium speed. Turn into a chafing dish and heat in the *blazer*. When simmering, keep hot by putting the blazer over the under pan in which you have enough hot water to make a little steam.

Sprinkle the bacon over the top, and serve with potato chips, Melba toast, crisp crackers or small toast triangles as a dunk.

HOT CLAM CHEESE DIP

1 10½-ounce can minced clams
¼ pound process cheese, cut in small pieces
1 small onion, finely chopped
3 tablespoons butter or margarine
½ green sweet pepper, diced
4 tablespoons catsup
1 tablespoon Worcestershire
1 tablespoon sherry (or milk)
¼ teaspoon Cayenne

Sauté onion and pepper in the butter or margarine 3 minutes. Add the rest of the ingredients and cook until the cheese melts, stirring constantly. Keep hot while you serve it, either in a chafing dish or in an earthenware casserole over a warmer. It must stay hot.

Serve with Melba toast, crisp crackers, or pumpernickel.

N.B. I have known a man who does not like clams to have seven dunks of this. Better serve small plates when you have the clam dip as it may drip off the crackers on your newly cleaned best rug. Worth it anyway.

CHEESE HOOIES

¼ pound butter
¼ pound strong American cheese
2 cups sifted flour
1 teaspoon salt
A good dash of Cayenne

Grate cheese into butter (I hope with a mouli grater). Cream well together, using a wooden spoon or your own clean hands. Add salt and Cayenne, then work in flour until thoroughly blended.

Knead on a board until smooth, roll into a long thin roll and put in the refrigerator to chill thoroughly. When chilled, slice thinly (use a sharp knife) and bake on a cookie sheet in a moderate oven (350°) until the hooies are beginning to brown (about 8-10 minutes).

Dust with powdered sugar.

Serve with cocktails, highballs, tomato juice, soup or salads.

N.B. This was the chief cooking specialty of my Virginia friend, Ida Fitzgerald. When she visited me in summer, we were not above a few cheese hooies with our breakfast coffee. She always doubled the recipe. They keep indefinitely, but are seldom allowed to.

CHICKEN LIVER NIBLETS

1 package frozen chicken livers
Flour to dredge
Garlic salt
Butter or margarine

Thaw the livers enough to separate them easily, then dredge with flour, sprinkle thoroughly with garlic salt. Sauté over medium heat in butter or margarine in a heavy saucepan until tender and brown.

Serve with cocktail picks.

Serves 4-6.

N.B. This is so easy and always a favorite. The garlic just does something to the livers.

CRAB CURRY CANAPÉ

1 medium or large can crabmeat
⅔ can cream of mushroom soup
2 tablespoons pimento, minced
¼ teaspoon curry powder (I use a little more)
¼ teaspoon salt

Heat in a double boiler or chafing dish. If it seems to be too thick, thin with a little cream. Serve in a bowl with crackers or crisp potato chips for dunking.

N.B. If you use frozen crabmeat, follow directions on the package for thawing and cooking (if uncooked). One package will equal a large-size can of crabmeat.

LOUELLA'S CUCUMBER DIP

1 pint commercial sour cream
1 tablespoon plus 1 teaspoon prepared horseradish
1 tablespoon paprika
1 tablespoon minced chives
1 teaspoon salt
1 teaspoon dill (fresh if you can get it)
¼ teaspoon garlic salt and monosodium glutonate
1 clove garlic, crushed
Freshly ground pepper
Basil vinegar to taste

Blend all ingredients together and chill at least an hour. The amount of basil vinegar depends on the sour cream, which varies in sharpness.

Serve in a bowl set in a larger bowl of crushed ice.

For the cucumber sticks, peel 4 large fresh cucumbers. Cut in thin strips and slice off the seedy part. Crisp them in ice water. Drain thoroughly.

N.B. Left-over dip, if there is any, makes a fine addition to your salad dressing.

FISH STICK NIBBLES

1 package frozen fish sticks
Grated American cheese

Cut fish sticks in thirds, roll in the cheese, and bake in a greased pan in a hot oven (425°) for 10 minutes. Arrange on a hot platter with a lettuce cup in the center filled with chili sauce or catsup. Place thin lemon wedges around the edge of the platter, and stick cocktail picks in each fish niblet.

Serves 4-6, depending on how many other canapés you have.

RED CAVIAR ISLAND

Red caviar
Cottage cheese, fine grain

Make a mound of the cottage cheese and frost it with the red caviar, leaving some of the cheese showing around the bottom edges.

Serve with Melba toast or crackers for dipping.

N.B. For the amount, suit yourself. But this is very popular and is so easy. The red caviar is milder than the black, and also less expensive. You may, if you are in the mood for it, squeeze a little lemon juice on the caviar. Or a bit of grated onion does no harm.

MUSHROOM CANAPÉS

16 large mushrooms
1 pound seasoned country sausage

Wipe mushrooms with a damp cloth. (I take a dim view of peeling them and taking away most of the flavor.) Remove the stems and save them for soup or gravy. Stuff the caps with the sausage and broil under low heat for 20 minutes. Lower the broiler rack if the fire is too hot.

Serve on rounds of buttered thin toast.

N.B. Thin toast should be thin. If you have regular sliced bread and do not own one of those tiger-toothed bread slicers, lay your bread flat on the counter, and put a piece of aluminum foil over the top. Then slide your sharpest knife through the center of the slice while keeping it in place with the foil, and there you are, I hope.

VERA'S PICKLED MUSHROOMS

1 large clove garlic, crushed
¾ cup salad oil
¼ cup olive oil
½ cup lemon juice
1 medium onion chopped (or 5 green onions, chopped)
1 teaspoon salt
¼ teaspoon pepper
½ teaspoon dry mustard
2 or 3 bay leaves
1 sprig fresh rosemary (½ teaspoon if dried)
½ teaspoon oregano
2 4-ounce cans big button mushrooms

Mix sauce, and taste for seasoning. Add dash of wine vinegar if desired. Pour into a jar with a top, add drained mushrooms, and cover. Store in the refrigerator at least 24 hours. Remove bay leaves after a few hours.

Drain on paper towels and stick a cocktail pick in each mushroom.

Serve with cocktails or on the hors d'oeuvre tray.

MUSHROOMS IN WINE

Fresh button mushrooms, 4 or 5 for each person to be served
Dry white wine
Olive oil
1 tablespoon finely chopped onion
1 tablespoon chopped chives
1 tablespoon chopped parsley
1 bay leaf
3 whole cloves
Pepper, Tabasco sauce (dash of this), salt
1 clove garlic

Cover the mushrooms with the wine and let stand in the refrigerator an hour. Then drain and cover the mushrooms with olive oil and put them in a jar. The seasonings above will serve for a pound of mushrooms. Add them to the jar and cover. Let stand 2 days in the refrigerator.

Serve with toothpicks for spearing.

HOT ONION CANAPÉS

Cut rounds of bread in bite-sized circles, using a small cooky cutter. Then cut very thin slices of onion to fit the rounds, and place a slice of onion on each.

Mix grated Parmesan cheese with mayonnaise (about 3 tablespoons cheese to a cup of mayonnaise). Top the onion slices with this mixture. Broil in a hot oven (400°) until the canapés are puffed up and beginning to brown.

Serve hot.

SNAPPY CHEESE BITS

Make up sandwiches with your favorite snappy cheese filling, and cut them into four triangles each. (Simply cut from corner to corner with a sharp knife.) Fry them in a skillet with plenty of butter or margarine, lift out with a spatula and serve on a hot platter.

Garnish with thin slivers of dill pickle.

RIPE OLIVES CURRIED

Heat the olives in their own liquor with curry powder added to taste. Serve hot or cold.

Eggs and Cheese

Sometimes i think if I were on a desert island and had a choice of just a few things to be shipwrecked with, I should take eggs and cheese. Eggs can be more varied in cooking than any other single thing. Cheese takes to every kind of dish from sprinkling on scrambled eggs to functioning as a dessert.

It may well be my one qualification for some hall of fame is that I no longer have to time eggs. I just feel when they are done. But when I was learning to cook, I had a hard time with eggs. I fried them to a stiff brown-papery shred. I boiled them until they were stiff as an old shoe sole. When I scrambled them, they were either soupy or a kind of pasteboard mat.

There is only one trick with eggs, and also with cheese. Be gentle. Keep the heat low. A quick sharp heat makes most egg and cheese dishes taste like a cast-off tire from a very old automobile. Both eggs and cheese continue cooking after you take them from the fire. Even a soft-boiled egg will keep cooking in the egg cup while you make the toast and finish the coffee. If you do not have a built-in mental timer, as I seem to have, get an egg timer. There are all sorts of directions about boiling eggs in every cookbook. I just toss the eggs in, preferably double-yolked ones, sometimes in cold water, sometimes in hot, and then I feel they are done, and they are. But until you get to feel like an egg, you are better off with a timer. These can be had at almost any ten cent store or hardware store.

The rule for cooking eggs is simple. You bring them to room temperature before you cook them. Otherwise they crack and some of the good egg leaches out. Cover with cold water and bring to a boil. Then turn the heat down and simmer. Twenty minutes for hard-cooked eggs.

Deviled eggs are the basis of many a dinner dish. It is now customary to hard-cook the eggs, cool them in cold water, shell, and cut in half lengthwise. Scoop out the yolk, mash in a bowl, and add mustard, mayonnaise, curry, or, whatever. I add whatever I have around from pickle relish to Hollandaise sauce.

You are better off with fresh eggs. An egg old enough to be on a pension never makes a good dish. When you break it, the yolk lies flat and watery, the white is thin. A fresh egg has an upstanding yolk, firm and golden, and the white is firm. The egg tends to hold its shape, even in a saucer. The white is not milky or cloudy, but clear.

With cheese, any dish is as good as the cheese in it. I remember the days of my childhood when we drove to the country to get green brick cheese, moist and tender and made by the Bavarians who settled in our country-side. Nowadays, there are many cheesemakers who will ship sound cheeses, and they are well worth it. I favor those made in Wisconsin where I grew up, just as I feel the delicate Wisconsin honey is particularly good.

But the store cheeses make fine dishes too, and are available in any grocery. Many of the process cheeses adapt themselves nicely to casseroles or sauces. The

Italian cheeses are now available in many stores and they have their place in a good cook's kitchen. Commercial grated cheese is a boon to quick meals, and it keeps. If you have no time to grate your own wedge of Parmesan, a shaker will help.

If you grate your own cheese, do not store it in a tight container as it will mold. Leave a little air space for it to breathe. I once grated several pounds of fresh cheese and put them in quart jars well-sealed. I lost every bit.

BAKED EGGS SPECIAL

    1 can cream-style corn (large size)
    4 green-pepper rings
    4 eggs
    Salt, pepper, paprika
    1 tablespoon crumbs
    2 tablespoons grated Parmesan cheese
    Butter or margarine

Season the corn with salt and pepper, and place in greased individual baking dishes or ramekins. Parboil the pepper rings 5 minutes and place a ring in each baking dish.

Break eggs into the rings, sprinkle with seasonings, crumbs and cheese. Dust with paprika. Bake 15 minutes in a moderate oven (350°).

Serves 4.

CREOLE EGGS

6 eggs, slightly beaten
1 tablespoon onion, diced
1 cup tomatoes, peeled and chopped
3 or 4 mushrooms, sliced
1 dessert spoon of capers, if desired
Butter or margarine

Sauté the onion and mushrooms in the butter or margarine until tender but not brown. Add the tomatoes and cook about 8 minutes. In a double boiler or chafing dish, pour the onion mixture, then add the eggs, capers and seasonings (use seasoned salt if you have it), paprika, a dash of Cayenne. Cook gently until the eggs are creamy, stirring (a wooden spoon is fine for this).

Serve over crisp crackers or buttered toast triangles.
Serves 4 to 5.

N.B. This is an easy, quick supper dish, and perfect for a chafing dish.

DEVILED EGGS CASSEROLE

6 hard-cooked eggs, deviled (see comment on eggs, p. 36)
16 shrimp, cooked
¾ cup sliced mushrooms
3 tablespoons butter or margarine
2 cups cheese sauce

Place the deviled eggs in a shallow greased baking pan. Break the shrimp in pieces and lay around the top of the eggs. Sauté the mushrooms in the butter or margarine; and when brown put on top of the shrimp. Pour the cheese sauce over, and bake in a moderate oven (350°) about 15 minutes or until it bubbles.

Serves 4-6.

CHEESE SAUCE:

2 tablespoons butter or margarine
2 tablespoons flour
½ teaspoon salt
2 cups milk
½ cup grated sharp cheese

Melt butter or margarine in a saucepan, stir in flour and salt, cook until smooth and free from lumps, stirring constantly, then gradually add milk and cheese and continue stirring until cheese is thoroughly blended and sauce bubbles.

EXTRA SPECIAL SCRAMBLED EGGS

2 eggs per person and an extra egg for the pan
Salt, pepper, paprika, pinch of chili powder
Cottage cheese, preferably the big curd

Beat the eggs in a bowl with a fork. Meanwhile melt butter or margarine in a heavy pan or chafing dish. When the butter is hot but not brown, turn the eggs in, and add the cottage cheese. You may use 2 tablespoons for 4 or 5 eggs, but the amount of cheese depends on how moist it is. A firm, creamed cottage cheese you use sparingly. A loose curd cheese you may be reckless with. Stir gently until the cheese is mixed through the eggs as they set. Turn the heat off before they are really done, for eggs keep on cooking.

N.B. The secret is to cook slowly over a low heat. After a time or two, you will know how much cheese your family likes in this creamy, delicate dish.

DAISY EGGS

1 egg to a person

Separate yolks from whites, keeping yolks unbroken and each yolk in a separate dish.

Beat whites well, and add seasoned salt, plenty of paprika, a dash of Worcestershire or A-1 sauce.

Put the whites in greased individual flat ramekins, or pile them in individual mounds on a baking sheet.

Slip the yolks carefully into the center of the beaten whites. Season with paprika and seasoned salt. Bake in a moderate oven (325°) until the yolks are firmly set.

EGGS MORNAY

6 eggs
2 tablespoons butter or margarine
2 tablespoons flour
2 cups milk
Salt, pepper, paprika to taste
Dash Tabasco or Worcestershire
1 teaspoon mild prepared mustard
⅓ cup Cheddar cheese, diced or grated

Melt the butter or margarine, blend in the flour and seasonings, and gradually add the milk, stirring constantly. When the sauce is smooth, add the cheese and stir until melted. Now put a layer of the cheese sauce in 3 greased individual baking dishes (or use a flat glass baking dish big enough to accommodate the 6 eggs). Slide 2 eggs into each ramekin on top of the sauce, cover partially with the remaining sauce, dust with paprika. Bake in a moderate oven (350°) 20 minutes or until the yolks are set, the sauce bubbly.

N.B. If you leave a little of each egg yolk showing, the eye appeal is greater. Tastes the same!

TAMALE SCRAMBLE

1 15½-oz. can tamales
8 eggs
1 cup milk
Salt
3 tablespoons butter or margarine
1½ cups grated cheese (Cheddar or American)

Take the husks from the tamales and cut each tamale in bite-size pieces. Place them in a baking dish and add the sauce from the can. Beat the eggs lightly and add milk and seasoning. Melt the butter or margarine in a skillet and add the egg mixture. Cook gently until the eggs begin to set. Pour the eggs over the tamales, top with the cheese and place the dish under the broiler (about 3-4 inches from the heat). When the cheese is melted, turn off the broiler and leave the dish in for two or three more minutes. Garnish with fresh sprigs of watercress.

Serves 4-5.

N.B. If you heat the tamales first, you can shorten the oven time.

TABASCO EGGS

1 cup thick cream
1 cup whole milk
1 teaspoon salt
Dash Cayenne and Tabasco to season
6 eggs
½ cup fine buttered bread crumbs
½ cup grated cheese, Parmesan or Cheddar

Heat in a chafing dish or ironware skillet, the cream and milk. Add salt, Cayenne, Tabasco.

When mixture is scalding, slip the eggs in one at a time, carefully. Keep the heat low if you are doing this on a range. As the eggs begin to set, sprinkle the crumbs and cheese over them. Keep dipping the sauce over the eggs until they are firmly set.

Serve on hot buttered toast.

Allow 2 eggs per person if this is the main dish.

N.B. This is a recipe I started housekeeping with, and it saved the day for me many a time.

STILLMEADOW CHEESE BAKE

6 slices white bread, with crusts removed
2½ cups grated Cheddar or Swiss cheese
3 eggs, beaten slightly
2½ cups milk
1 teaspoon salt
Pepper to taste
Dry mustard (½ to 1 teaspoon)

Lay the bread in a greased baking pan, spreading each slice with butter or margarine and fitting one layer in the pan. Sprinkle the cheese over the bottom layer, add the mustard, lay another layer of bread over this, and then pour over the eggs mixed with the milk and seasonings.

Let stand an hour. Bake in a slow oven (325°) 30 to 40 minutes, or until it puffs up and begins to brown. If a straw inserted in the center comes out clean, it is done.

Serves 3-4.

N.B. You may increase the bread slices and cheese and add 1 extra egg with ½ cup more milk to serve 6.

QUICHE LORRAINE

Pastry to line a 10-inch pie tin (see pastry recipe or use a pastry mix as directed). Line the pan with pastry. Prick with a fork on the bottom. Chill until you make the filling.

1 cup grated Swiss cheese (use a mouli rotary grater if you have one)
4 eggs, slightly beaten
2 cups thin or thick cream
1 pinch Cayenne
1 pinch sugar
1 teaspoon salt, and pepper to taste
1 white onion
Bacon or cooked ham

Spread the surface of the pastry with soft butter. Beat eggs and cream together until blended. Add the seasonings, and stir lightly. Meanwhile grill a dozen slices of bacon, break in bits and sprinkle on the crust. Sauté a small diced onion in butter or margarine until transparent. Sprinkle on the crust. Then sprinkle the cheese on. Pour the egg mixture over. Bake in a hot oven (450°) for 12 minutes, reduce to (325°) and bake until a knife inserted in the middle comes out clean. For most ovens 25 minutes is enough.

Serves 4, but 3 will finish it. For 6-8 persons, I make two pies.

N.B. You may omit the bacon and onion, or you may substitute chopped cooked ham for them. I happen to like the bacon and onion best.

Serve with a green vegetable such as fresh peas cooked with mint leaf, broccoli (no Hollandaise this time) or spinach. Add a fruit salad and coffee and skip dessert as this is a rich dinner.

Quiche Lorraine freezes beautifully. Freeze after baking. I first had Quiche Lorraine at Rose Feld's, when we both were celebrating successful new books. Most of the time as we ate the whole Lorraine, we talked about food, not books. I copied down the recipe as we sat by the fire drinking hot black coffee and watching the moonlight silvering the wide floor boards.

MEXICAN RABBIT

3 tablespoons butter or margarine
1 onion, chopped
½ green pepper, chopped
2 tablespoons flour
1 cup milk
2 cups grated Cheddar cheese
1½ cups stewed tomatoes (or 1 medium can)
Salt, cayenne
2 egg yolks, beaten

Sauté the onion and pepper in the butter or margarine in the top pan of a chafing dish. Put the pan over hot water, add the flour and stir until blended. Then add the milk and stir until smooth. Add the cheese, and when it has melted, add tomatoes and seasonings. Cook for 10 minutes, stirring occasionally, then add the egg yolks and stir for 2 minutes.

Serve on hot toast points.

Serves 4.

SWISS CHEESE FONDUE

1 pound Swiss cheese, cut in small cubes
Flour (potato flour if possible)
½ bottle dry white wine
2 tablespoons kirsch, if desired, or brandy or bourbon
Garlic

Dredge the cheese lightly in the flour. Rub the inside of an earthenware casserole with the garlic. Place the pot in a pan of hot water—or in the bottom pan of a chafing dish, with water enough to cover the bottom of the pan. Pour the wine in, heat to boiling point, add the cheese, and stir until the cheese melts. Season to taste with salt, freshly ground pepper. Add the kirsch when the Fondue is smooth and creamy. Serve in the casserole. Pieces of French bread must be served with it, and long forks for dipping. Guests spear the bread and dip into the casserole.

Keep the casserole warmed.

Serves 4.

WELSH RABBIT

2 tablespoons butter
3 cups Cheddar cheese, grated
½ teaspoon dry mustard
½ teaspoon salt
1 teaspoon Worcestershire
pinch Cayenne
2 egg yolks, lightly beaten
½ cup ale or beer
Crisp buttered toast

In a double boiler or chafing dish, melt the butter, add the cheese and stir with a wooden spoon in one direction only. When the cheese melts, add the seasonings. Combine the egg yolks with the ale, and add gradually, stirring constantly. Do not let it boil. When piping hot, pour on the toast and serve immediately.

Serves 2-4.

CHEESE SOUFFLÉ

    4 egg yolks
    5 egg whites, beaten until stiff
    1 cup crumbled or grated cheese (Cheddar, American, or
        Swiss)
    2 tablespoons butter or margarine
    2 tablespoons flour
    ¾ cup milk
    Dash Worcestershire
    Salt (taste for this as some cheese is strong), pepper, paprika

Melt the butter or margarine over medium heat, blend in the flour. Add milk gradually, and stir until smooth, adding the seasonings as you stir. Remove the pan from the fire and beat the egg yolks in, one at a time, alternately adding the cheese. Put back on the range over low heat and stir until the cheese melts. Remove from stove and let cool a few minutes. Then fold in the egg whites (with a wooden spoon if you have one).

Bake in an ungreased quart casserole in a moderate oven (350°) for about 45 minutes, or until the soufflé begins to draw away from the sides of the casserole and the top is delicately browned.

Serves 3-4.

N.B. Serve with crisp buttered toast points, asparagus, a mixed green salad with a light French dressing, coffee. Add catsup, chili sauce or Sauce Diable for those who wish a dribble on the soufflé.

GNOCCHI

    1 cup cornmeal (preferably white, but yellow will do)
    ¾ cup grated Parmesan cheese
    3 cups cold water
    2 teaspoons dry mustard
    1 egg, beaten
    Salt
    Freshly ground pepper
    ⅓ cup melted butter or margarine
    ⅓ cup grated Parmesan cheese
    4 medium tomatoes
    2 packages brown-and-serve sausages

Put the water and salt in a deep saucepan and bring to boil. Stir in the cornmeal slowly, stirring constantly. Continue to stir and cook until the cornmeal is thickened and creamy. It will begin to draw from the sides of the pan when it is done. Then cover, and reduce heat to low, and cook 10 minutes.

Remove from heat, stir in cheese, mustard, egg, salt, pepper. Turn into a greased 10 x 6 x 2 baking dish, smoothing it evenly with a spatula. Set in the refrigerator until 15-20 minutes before dinner. Then cut the Gnocchi into squares and arrange in the center of a large flat baking dish (or metal skillet). Top with the ⅓ cup of grated cheese and the melted butter or margarine.

Start the broiler in the range. While it heats, cut the tomatoes in wedges and arrange at one end of the dish. Sprinkle with seasonings and remaining cheese. Broil 5 minutes, then add the sausages at the opposite end of the dish and continue broiling until sausages are brown, cheese bubbly.

    Serves 6.

N.B. Tomatoes and sausages may be omitted.

Soups

WHEN I WAS GROWING UP, Mama always had the soup kettle simmering on the back of the big range in winter. Soup brings memories to me of snowy dusks when I dumped my ice skates in the hall and flew into the kitchen, sniffing to see what kind of soup I could dish a pre-dinner bowl of. After sleigh rides, my beau and I could devour such a quantity of chowder or oyster stew that we only had room for two or three pieces of deep-dish apple pie.

Nobody else heard of summer soups in those days, so far as I know, but we had them. After a hot morning at tennis, how good the jellied beef and chicken soups tasted. These were generally used to carry to sick people in earthenware bowls covered with white linen napkins, but in our house, we just liked soup, well or sick.

I favored, and still do, soup with lots of things in it. A clear consommé is for dieting, but a consommé with homemade noodles or croutons dusted with Parmesan and paprika, or with a few, not many, tiny peas or tips of asparagus—well, that is something else again! Jellied consommé takes a happy view of crisp cool cucumber stars, paper-thin slices of lemon sprinkled with paprika and chopped parsley. And a robust winter-night supper soup needs parsley dumplings or a lacing of croutons done in garlic butter.

The base of a homemade soup is soundly set on the soup bone. Marrow bones are best, veal or beef or both, but I toss in chop bones, rib-roast bones, lamb shanks, ham bones, chicken bones, turkey bones. For cooking them I do not favor the pressure cooker, unless I am in a hurry. Slow simmer is the trick. I cover them with fresh cold water, add a handful of celery tops, some diced onion, a leek or so, if I have one, a little parsley, a few bay leaves, four or five cloves, a dash of pickling spice (much under-rated for general cooking), plenty of seasoned salt, freshly ground pepper, and a carrot or two. I add a clove of garlic or some garlic powder and a little celery seed. Then I go about my business and let the kettle simmer slowly along. At night, in winter, I put it in the wood-shed where it can get really cold. In summer, I have to take everything else out of the refrigerator to make room for it in all manner of bowls and pans. It must cool to be skimmed of the fat. The fat goes in the cockers' breakfast. This stock should practically stand alone when done. If it is watery after being thoroughly chilled, you need to simmer again and add another veal knuckle or beef shank.

Now when you feel in the mood for soup, you strain out the flavoring vegetables and start fresh. Leave the bones in (there might be one last bit of richness there) add whatever vegetables you wish, and rice, noodles, macaroni, pasta sea shells and so on, adding each in-gredient according to how long it takes to cook. You do not want mush. Many people overcook the soup vege-tables and that may be why some of them do not like soup!

Practically any vegetable can go in the soup kettle, but be wary of parsnips, as they tend to sweeten the brew. You will need more onion, more carrots, and the rest of the celery stalk, cut in pieces. You do need tomatoes, either fresh or canned. Peas and beans, potatoes, turnips (slice them thin), and whatever you have around. Taste. When the soup is well on the way, add some tomato paste, a spoonful of beef extract or chicken to reinforce the richness. Add the rice or barley or macaroni or noodles. Add a dash of chili if it seems bland. And some of my best soups came from adding left-over mashed potatoes and a bowl of left-over spaghetti! A can or so of mushrooms helps too.

Then fish out the bones, drop in the dumplings, cover and cook ten minutes. Heat the soup bowls, and there you are.

Parsley dumplings are easily made from a mix, with chopped parsley stirred in. Cheese dumplings go the same way with grated cheese. If you use a mix, follow the directions on the package. There is a new theory whereby you cook them uncovered 10 minutes, then cover for 10. In my life with dumplings, I cover and leave them alone for 15 minutes, then peek carefully. The soup must be boiling as you drop them in.

Marrow dumplings are a special touch, if you have 3 tablespoons of marrow. Mix them with ½ cup dry bread crumbs, some chopped parsley, salt, freshly grated pepper, a bit of grated lemon rind. Add 2 beaten eggs, and blend. Form into small balls and drop into the boiling stock, cover, boil for 4 minutes or until they float to the surface.

A last word about soups, before I give some other-than-beef-stock recipes. I learned from a Jamaican friend to make a delicious soup with only vegetables, such as dried limas, peas, lentils, and so on. Iris would buy a handful of greens for 10 cents and maybe one fresh tomato. This was during the depression when food was hard to buy cheaply. She soaked the dried beans or whatever overnight, cooked them in the morning. Then she added the fresh vegetables, and a generous dollop of butter or margarine. If she had it, she added a chicken bouillon cube or two. If not, she added more butter or margarine (it was always margarine) and seasonings. A few left-over baked beans might go in, or a small dish of canned peas (left-over). The result was a soup that seemed as rich as if a whole beef knuckle had been the basis.

One final note—hot soup should be hot as a volcano. Cold soup should be ice-cold. There is no Mr. In-between for soup!

CHEDDAR SOUP

¾ cup Cheddar, grated
1 tablespoon onion, chopped
1 tablespoon butter or margarine
1 tablespoon flour
1 cup chicken stock or consommé
2 cups milk

Melt butter or margarine, add the onion and cook until golden. Blend in the flour, then add the chicken stock and milk, stirring. Bring to boiling, add cheese, and stir until cheese is melted.

Garnish with chopped parsley or chives or croutons.

Serves 6.

QUICK BORSCH

1 No. 2 can beets (shredded)
1 teaspoon minced onion
1½ cups beef stock or bouillon
1 cup water
Salt and pepper to taste
1 tablespoon lemon juice, fresh, canned or frozen
Sour cream

Drain the beets, reserving the juice. Combine the juice, onion, bouillon, water; add the beets and cook for about 5 minutes, or until simmering. Add seasonings and lemon juice. Pour into hot soup bowls and top each bowl with a spoonful of sour cream.

Serves 4-6.

N.B. If you use whole beets, shred them on your biggest grater (as for cole slaw).

This is an excellent first course for dinner, especially a mixed-grill platter of lamb chops, tiny broiled sausages, grilled pineapple slices, and sliced cooked sweet potatoes brushed with butter or margarine and broiled just as the chops are about done.

NEW ENGLAND CLAM CHOWDER

2 dozen hardshell clams in the shell (or 3 dozen if small)
¼ pound salt pork
1 minced onion
2 cups raw sliced or diced potatoes
3 tablespoons flour
3 tablespoons butter or margarine
4 cups milk
Parsley, salt, paprika, pinch of dry thyme

Scrub the clams well in several waters with a firm brush. Put them in a deep kettle and pour over 1 cup water. Steam, tightly covered, until the shells open.

Remove the clams and chop the hard portions with a sharp knife (or use a food chopper).

Strain the juice through cheesecloth and add 2 cups water.

Meanwhile dice the salt pork and heat over a low flame until it is crisp and golden brown. Add the onion and cook until the onion is transparent. Add the hard part of the clams.

Cook slowly for five minutes.

Sprinkle the flour over and add clam juice and water. Next add the potatoes, cover, and simmer until the potatoes are done. Add the soft part of the clams and the butter, and when the chowder comes to a boil add the milk (heated but not boiling).

Add seasonings.

Let the chowder ripen at least half an hour. Serve hot with toasted chowder crackers.

Serves 6.

N.B. You may use 2 cans minced clams. You may also use part light cream for a richer chowder. You will, if you are sensible, float an extra dollop of butter on top and more paprika.

HERMAN SMITH'S BOUILLABAISSE

    3 lbs. fresh-water fish, in serving pieces (keep heads)
    1 can shrimp (8 ounce)
    1 can lobster (medium or large)
    4 cups water
    2 onions, sliced
    3 leeks, sliced
    1 large clove garlic, mashed
    ½ cup oil
    2 tomatoes, peeled and chopped
    Pinch saffron
    1 strip orange rind
    1 bay leaf
    4 whole cloves
    6 peppercorns
    1 cup dry white table wine
    6 slices toast
    1 clove garlic, cut in half
    3 tablespoons soft butter or margarine
    3 tablespoons chopped chives
    2 tablespoons butter or margarine, melted
    1 tablespoon parsley, minced

Cook fish heads and liquid from shrimp and lobster for 10 minutes. Drain, reserve stock. Cook onions, leek and garlic in hot oil until soft. Add 4 cups reserved stock, tomatoes, saffron, orange rind.

Tie bay leaf, cloves, peppercorns in cheesecloth bag and add to mixture. Simmer about 30 minutes. Then remove the bag, and add fish and shrimp and cook about 10 minutes more. Then add the wine. Rub the toast with the cut garlic, spread with soft butter and sprinkle with chives. Heat the lobster in butter or margarine and place a spoonful on each slice of toast in deep soup plates. Pour in the stew, sprinkle with parsley and serve at once.

Serves 6.

N.B. Or you may put the stew in the soup plates and lay

the lobster toast on top. *This is a complete dinner, but have extra toast ready for dunking. A tossed salad goes well. When Herman Smith last came to see me, he was carried out of the car. But his gay and gentle spirit never flagged and it was a joy to visit with him. His writing was gay and gentle too, and his cooking was beyond description. I admit I am not much at cooking fish heads, but as long as Herman said to cook them, they were to be cooked.*

CREAM OF CHICKEN AND CUCUMBER SOUP

1 can cream of mushroom soup, diluted with ½ can water
1 can cream of chicken soup, diluted with ½ can water
1 cup peeled and diced cucumber
2 tablespoons butter or margarine
2 tablespoons grated onion
¼ teaspoon curry powder
½ cup top milk or light cream
Salt, pepper, paprika to taste

Melt butter or margarine in a deep kettle, add curry, onion and cucumber. Simmer, covered, until the cucumber is tender (5 minutes or less). Add the soups and the cream and heat to simmering, but do not boil. Season to taste and serve at once in warm soup bowls.

Serves 4-6.

N.B. You may like more curry, but taste after adding. On a broiling August day, try this served frosty cold with a sprig of watercress in each bowl. To complete the meal, if the soup is hot, serve grapefruit and orange salad, adding a bit of mayonnaise to a French dressing to pour over. Tiny hot biscuits (use the smallest cutter or the center of a doughnut cutter) and currant jelly go well, winter or summer. Make the coffee hot or the tea iced according to the time. In summer, our choice is a Chef's Salad with fresh crisp mixed greens, slivers of tongue, chicken, ham, Swiss cheese, minced scallions.

CORN CHOWDER

1 can cream-style corn (medium size)
2 slices salt pork, diced
1 small onion, diced
2 medium potatoes, peeled and diced
2 cups water
2 cups light cream or top milk

In a heavy kettle fry the salt pork to a light brown (add no fat) and then the onion. Cook gently until the onion is golden, then add the potatoes and season with freshly ground pepper and salt, and add the water. Cook until the potatoes are tender but not mushy. Meanwhile heat the cream or milk but do not boil. Add with the corn to the first mixture, and re-heat to simmering (no boiling).

Serves 4-6.

N.B. This is a robust supper soup. Serve in a warm tureen with a good dusting of paprika and a little chopped parsley on top. With it serve crisp cucumber slices and chilled tomato slices dressed with a light French dressing. Add crusty French bread cut in chunks and spread with garlic butter.

JELLIED CUCUMBER SOUP

1½ cups peeled, seeded, diced cucumber
4 cups chicken broth (no fat, please)
2 envelopes unflavored gelatin
¼ cup cold water
¼ cup lemon juice, fresh, canned or frozen
A few drops green vegetable coloring
Salt, pepper, paprika to taste

Heat the broth to boiling. Soften the gelatin in the cold water and add to the broth, then add lemon juice and coloring. Season well. Cool until it begins to thicken, then add the cucumber and chill again until set. At serving time, break it up with a fork and serve in chilled cups or bowls. Garnish with lemon slices dusted with paprika. (Use the Hungarian sweet Paprika if you can get it.)
Serves 4-6.

N.B. This is a cool, light luncheon soup and low in calories too. Makes a fine prelude to a cold buffet. Or serve sliced cold chicken, tongue, turkey, or cold cuts and ripe tomatoes stuffed with cottage cheese. Fill the bread basket with rye or pumpernickel. Add tall glasses of strong iced tea.

LOBSTER CHOWDER

1 medium-sized lobster, boiled
3 tablespoons butter or margarine
¼ cup cracker crumbs
4 cups top milk (or 3 cups milk and 1 cup thin cream)
1 medium onion, diced
1 cup chicken or clam broth
Seasonings

Cut the meat from the lobster in small pieces. Cream the butter or margarine with the green liver of the lobster and the crumbs. Meanwhile scald the milk with the onion, and strain into the first mixture.

Cook the shell of the lobster in the broth for about 10 minutes and strain into the milk. Add lobster meat and re-heat, but do not boil. Season with seasoned salt, paprika, and a spoonful of sherry, if desired.

Serves 4-6.

N.B. You may use frozen lobster or a large can of lobster.

POOR MAN'S STEW

3 medium potatoes, peeled and diced
4 slices salt pork, diced
4 medium onions, chopped or cut fine
1½ quarts water
Pepper to taste

Fry the salt pork in a heavy deep kettle until crisp and brown. When the pork is nearly done, add the onions, and when the onions are golden add the water and potatoes. Simmer, covered, until the potatoes are tender. Add pepper. Then drop in dumplings, cover and cook 15 minutes.

DUMPLINGS

2 cups biscuit mix
2 tablespoons parsley flakes

Mix as directed on the package.
Serves 4-5.

N.B. You may use part chicken broth or beef stock in place of the water, but this is delicious as is.

We first had it during a February blizzard, when "the electric" was off. We did not dare open the deep-freeze with the current off, and the shelves were pretty bare after a three-day storm. A guest from Vermont asked if we had any salt pork . . . We hung the iron soup kettle over the fire in the fireplace, and shortly the wonderful smell of salt pork and onions filled the house. That was a memorable dinner, that one. We served cole slaw (plenty of cabbage stored in the cellar), coffee (boiled with an egg shell dropped in it), and for dessert rosy Delicious apples and Port Salut cheese.

MINESTRONE

  1½ quarts beef stock
  ½ lb. salt pork, diced
  1 package frozen peas
  ½ lb. frozen lima beans
  ½ head medium-sized cabbage, shredded
  ½ lb. fresh spinach, cut fine
  3 medium-sized carrots, diced
  2 stalks celery, cut fine
  1 medium onion, diced
  2 cloves garlic, chopped
  2 tomatoes, cut in small pieces
  ¼ cup raw brown or long-grain white rice
  1 tablespoon chopped parsley
Salt and pepper and paprika to taste

Bring the stock to a boil. Meanwhile lightly fry the salt pork, just until it turns color but is not brown. Add the salt pork and the remaining ingredients to the stock, reduce the heat and simmer gently until the vegetables are tender.
Serves 4-6.

N.B. Serve with a bowl of grated Parmesan cheese, or stir the cheese right into the soup (about ½ a cup). Serve in soup plates. This soup is too thick for dunking, but stick with the Italian bread (wrapped in aluminum foil and heated to piping).

I have eaten Minestrone in any number of Italian restaurants and have yet to find it twice the same. The only thing I find is, that it is always better than the last. I think you may add almost any vegetables, from chick peas to fresh green beans. Kidney beans are fine too. I use canned and add juice and all, but this is no doubt unethical. If you are short on rice, elbow macaroni does no harm. I do not know the origin of Minestrone but I always suspect an Italian housewife had a good soup bone simmering half the day, and just tossed in whatever she had because there was not money enough to buy veal for Parmigiana for a large and very hungry family.

If you have a country garden, it is quite possible to find a few pods of okra, a Brussels sprout or so, and even a few slivers of turnip in that soup.

CREAMY ONION SOUP

4 medium onions, sliced
2 tablespoons olive oil
2 tablespoons butter or margarine
2 cups chicken broth
1 cup cream
Salt, pepper, to taste
Parsley, chopped
Parmesan cheese, grated

Cook the onions in the olive oil and butter or margarine until golden but not brown. Add the broth and cream. Bring just to boiling point, but do not boil. Top with the parsley and serve with grated Parmesan cheese.

Serves 4.

N.B. Serve hot buttered crackers dusted with paprika with this, and any kind of salad at all, except onion and orange!

We like this as a change from the customary French onion soup, and it is substantial enough for a one-dish supper.

SHIRLEY BOOTH'S PURÉE MONGOLE

  1 can cream of tomato soup, condensed
  1 can cream of green pea soup, condensed
  2 cans top milk or thin cream
  1 tablespoon sherry

Heat the two soups with the milk or cream until just simmering, but not boiling. Add the sherry. Serve in heated soup bowls or mugs.

Serves 4-5.

N.B. The reason we now call this Shirley's soup is that when we were discussing recipes, she said she made this soup one time, and it was good. She couldn't think how she had dreamed it up, and then it burst over her that she read it in my Diary! I think the soup people originally thought of it, but from now on, it is Shirley's soup to us.

We like it with croutons (add garlic salt to the butter or margarine you fry them in) and a gelatin fruit salad with sour cream and mayonnaise dressing. No dessert, unless the green and white grapes just happen to be ready to pick.

SPAGHETTI SOUP

 1 large soup bone, veal, beef or lamb, preferably with some
   meat on it
 8 bay leaves
 2 or 3 whole cloves
 1 cup sliced onions
 2 teaspoons salt; freshly ground pepper to taste
 1 No. 2 can tomatoes
 1 pound spaghetti

Cover the soup bone with cold water. Add the first 4 ingredients and when the soup comes to a boil, add the tomatoes. Turn the heat low, and simmer 2 or 3 hours. Taste for
seasoning, and if the stock is not rich enough add 1 dessert-
spoonful of beef concentrate or 2 bouillon cubes.

When it is time to eat, cook the spaghetti in rapidly boiling
water, salted, until tender but not mushy.

Heap the spaghetti, at serving time, in big warm soup
plates, and pour the soup over. You may remove the bay
leaves and cloves by straining the soup.

Serve with a big bowl of grated Parmesan cheese.

Serves 8.

*N.B. If you use a pressure cooker for 3 pound bones, 2 quarts
water, cook at 10 pounds pressure for 40 minutes.*

*You may add garlic salt, a dash of chili powder, ½ can
tomato paste, a dash or so of Worcestershire or what you will.
But serve only a green salad and a lot of crusty French bread
for sopping.*

MURRAY EDWARDS' VICHYSSOISE

2 cups diced raw potatoes
2 cups diced raw leeks or onions (leeks are better)
1 cup chicken broth
1 cup sour cream
1 teaspoon Worcestershire
Salt to taste
Chopped chives

Cook potatoes and leeks in a very little water until soft. Press through a food mill, or use your blender. Add the broth. Let cool. Then add the sour cream and beat well. Add seasonings and chill.

Serve in individual cups, topped with the chives.

Serves 4-5.

N.B. I have tried many variations of Vichyssoise, and this is my true love as far as this soup goes. I first had it at dinner in Murray's house on the Virginia Military Institute grounds. I knew at the first spoonful that a colonel can cook for me any day. Afterward we sat on the back veranda and watched the sun go down over the blue Virginia mountains while we sipped the Colonel's own specially ground coffee.

WATERCRESS SOUP

2 cups chopped fresh watercress
½ package Old English style Process cheese, sliced thin
2 tablespoons butter or margarine
2 tablespoons flour
4 cups top milk
Salt and pepper to taste

Melt the butter or margarine, blend in the flour, add the milk gradually, stirring constantly over a medium heat. When it begins to thicken, add the cheese, and stir until the cheese is melted and the soup is smooth.

Add seasonings and the watercress and cook 2 or 3 minutes longer. Serve at once.

Serves 4.

N.B. Try this as that one hot dish needed with a cold supper, particularly good with cold thinly-sliced ham and a fresh vegetable salad, and wedges of French or Italian bread (heat the bread in the oven first).

Fish and Shellfish

I LIKE TO SIT QUIETLY in the canoe, dangling a line, and just wait for the proper fish to find the bait. Flounder is my favorite, and for that a quiet Cape Cod cove is best. Sky and water are all of a piece. Little sailboats pearl the horizon. Grey gulls ride the air currents. When the creel is decently heavy, we paddle ashore and Jill cleans and fillets the shining fish while I stand by with seasoned flour and a frying pan. I use half butter and half margarine, by the way, for fish frying. (Margarine burns less quickly, butter gives extra flavor.)

Fish you catch yourself has added to it the savor of the day itself, and, seasoned with sun, garnished with happy memories, it is fit for a royal table.

Next best is a trip to the wharf when lobster boats come in. I point a finger for my choice, but never venture to pick up a lobster. The one time Jill was not around to do the boiling, I dropped the lobster in the paper bag into the boiling sea water; I doubt whether any other lobster was ever seasoned with boiled paper bag.

But even buying frozen or canned fish can be fun, for here in our village the Food Center is a center for more than food. It is an informal social club where neighbors stop to talk, and all the news of interest is gathered. The big bulletin board is the local newspaper, advising us of the Lions' Club Clam Bake, The Ladies Aid Ham and Bean Supper, the Square Dance, and the benefit movie at the high school.

If I were to define the word Fish for the Dictionary, I should put—FISH: That which must never be over-cooked!

FILLET BORLANDIA

Fillets of flounder, whitefish or haddock, fresh or frozen, 2 to each person
Creole sauce, canned (1 can for 4-5 fillets)
Salt, pepper, oregano to taste

Dry fillets thoroughly on paper towels. Lay them in a greased baking dish, cover with the sauce. Sprinkle the seasonings lightly over. Bake in a hot (400°) oven until the fillets are tender when tested with a fork. The time will vary from 25 to 40 minutes depending on whether you use frozen or fresh fillets.

N.B. Spaghetti sauce may be substituted, or canned mushroom sauce. Or if you have time you may make your own Creole sauce.

Serve with baked potatoes or fluffy rice and a tossed salad and coffee. Keep dessert light; a fruit compote is best.

BAKED FILLETS WITH LOBSTER SAUCE

1 package frozen flounder or sole fillets
1 can frozen lobster soup (or shrimp soup)
Butter or margarine
Freshly ground pepper
Chopped parsley

Separate the fillets and lay them in a greased flat baking dish. Thaw the soup by immersing it in hot water until it sloshes in the can when you shake it. (Or you can thaw it in a sunny windowsill in 2 hours, if you happen to think of it.)

Pour the soup over the fillets, add pepper and parsley. Bake in a medium oven (350°) until the fish is tender when you pierce it with a fork and the soup is reduced to a creamy sauce.

Serves 2-4.

N.B. Serve garnished with fresh watercress. Add a tossed salad made with plain French dressing (the fish will be rich) and pass wedges of hot crusty French bread for sopping up that sauce. If you must have a vegetable, use tiny canned peas with half a can of mushrooms added. And to top off a meal that almost does itself, serve canned grapefruit sections with a dash of crème de menthe and a sprig of fresh mint dipped in powdered sugar. Keep the coffee hot.

JANET'S FILLET OF SOLE

1 package frozen fillets of sole or flounder
1 lb. fresh or 1 package frozen spinach
Parmesan cheese, grated
Sauce
Croutons

Cover the bottom of a casserole with the spinach, cooked and seasoned.

Lay seasoned fillets over the spinach and sprinkle well with the cheese. Pour the sauce over, sprinkle again with cheese and add croutons. Bake in a moderate (375°) oven for 25 minutes or until golden brown.

THE SAUCE:

Melt 2 tablespoons butter or margarine, blend in 2 tablespoons flour, add 1 cup canned consommé and cook until thickened. Season to taste and add ½ cup cream (evaporated milk if the cream is gone). Stir well, remove from fire. (Or use Béchamel Sauce recipe in SAUCE section.)

Serves 2-4.

SEAFOOD BORLANDIA

Fillets, frozen or fresh, flounder or whitefish, 2 to a person
Oysters, fresh or frozen, 4 to a person. (A container of
  frozen serves 4)
Shrimp, 1 6-oz. can to 4 persons
Cheese sauce

Place drained fillets in a greased casserole or baking dish,
add the raw oysters, then the shrimp. For the sauce, make a
cream sauce (see SAUCES) and add ¼ cup grated Cheddar
cheese. Pour over the fish, and bake in a moderate (350°) oven
for 30-40 minutes, depending on whether fillets are frozen or
fresh. Test with a fork. When the fillets are flaky, and the
sauce bubbly, dinner is ready.

*N.B. Serve with garlic buttered French or Italian bread and
a green salad. Pass a bowl of frosty white grapes for dessert,
or ripe peaches.*

DEVILED SALMON

1 large can salmon, flaked and with skin removed
1 cup canned tomato soup, undiluted
¼ onion
¼ green pepper, diced
3 tablespoons butter
1 teaspoon salt
1 teaspoon prepared mustard
1 slice lemon with peel

Put in a blender and blend well. (Or mince onion, pepper, lemon very fine.)

Pour the tomato mix over the salmon and stir. Pile in greased ramekins. Top each ramekin with buttered crumbs and a thin slice of lemon. Dust with paprika. Bake in a hot oven until bubbly (about 25 minutes).

Serves 4.

SHAD ROE WITH TOAST TRIANGLES

2 pounds fresh shad roe (or 3 cans roe)
½ cup butter or margarine
Salt, pepper, monosodium glutamate, paprika
3 or 4 slices bread

In a chafing dish or skillet, heat the butter, but do not let
it brown. Lay the fresh roe in, cover, and cook over low heat
about twelve minutes or until it is tender. Turn once. Add
butter or margarine if it gets dry. Heat canned roe in butter.

Arrange toast triangles on a heated platter and lay roe on
top. Season to taste and arrange lemon wedges sprinkled with
paprika around the platter.

Serves 6.

N.B. *When the shad roe man comes down our road, we
buy six or twelve. Roe freezes very well. But when the shad
are not in season, the canned roe is excellent. It makes a
special Sunday breakfast as well as a fine supper dish.*

SOLE BAKED IN WINE SAUCE

2 pounds sole or flounder fillets
2 tablespoons lemon juice
2 tablespoons dry white wine
Salt and pepper
4 tablespoons butter or margarine
4 tablespoon flour (¼ cup)
2 cups milk
¼ teaspoon freshly ground pepper
½ teaspoon dry mustard
1 teaspoon Worcestershire
½ teaspoon tarragon, crumbled
2 tablespoons each, chopped green pepper, parsley, chives
2 tablespoons grated Parmesan cheese
4 tablespoons dry sherry

Sprinkle fillets with lemon juice, wine, salt and pepper. Chill several hours.

Melt butter in a saucepan, blend in flour. When smooth add milk slowly, and stir over low heat until thick. Add the pepper, mustard, Worcestershire, tarragon, green pepper, chives, parsley, cheese and sherry.

Arrange fillets in a flat casserole or baking pan (greased) and pour the sauce over.

Bake in a moderate oven (350°) for 30 minutes, or until fish flakes with a fork.

Serves 6.

TUNA AVOCADO PIE

Pastry for a 9-inch pie plate
¼ cup grated Parmesan cheese

2 cans tuna
1 avocado, peeled, pitted and cut into 1-inch cubes
1 chicken bouillon cube
½ cup boiling water
¼ cup butter or margarine
2 tablespoons finely chopped onion
¼ cup flour
¾ cup heavy cream
1 tablespoon lemon juice
¼ cup chili sauce
Salt; chopped parsley to taste
½ cup shredded Swiss cheese

Make your usual recipe for pastry, but add the Parmesan cheese to the flour first. Line the 9-inch pan with the pastry. Drain the tuna and break into bite-size pieces. Dissolve the bouillon cube in boiling water. Meanwhile, melt butter or margarine in a skillet, sauté the onion in it, then blend in the flour. Add bouillon and cream, stirring constantly until thickened, then the lemon juice, chili sauce, seasonings, tuna and avocado.

Mix all together well and pour into the pie shell. Sprinkle with the Swiss cheese and bake in a hot oven (400°) 25-30 minutes or until filling is bubbly and crust is brown.

Serves 6.

LOIS KLAKRING'S BAKED TUNA CASSEROLE

¼ cup shortening—butter, margarine, vegetable
1 teaspoon minced onion
1 tablespoon minced green pepper
4 tablespoons flour
1 teaspoon salt
½ teaspoon paprika
2 cups milk
2 teaspoons chopped pimento
2 7-ounce cans tuna
Buttered bread crumbs

Sauté onion and pepper in fat about 2 minutes. Add flour, salt, paprika, and blend. Add milk gradually and cook until thickened, stirring constantly. Add pimento. Separate tuna into flakes. Mix bread crumbs in melted butter or margarine. Arrange alternate layers of sauce, tuna and crumbs in a greased casserole. Top with crumbs and bake, covered, at 375° or moderately hot oven for about 30 minutes. It will bubble when it is done, and the top will be brown.

Serves 4-6, but 3 can do a good job of it, and never mind.

N.B. Serve with a grapefruit and avocado salad and lemon juice in the French dressing. Hot buttermilk biscuits do no harm, and you can buy these ready to bake. Don't bother with dessert, unless you have some of the Wisconsin Port Salut to serve with toasted crackers. But double the coffee.

CAPE COD CLAM PIE

1 pint raw clams, including liquor, or an equal amount of
frozen clams, thawed
2 tablespoons butter or margarine
1 tablespoon flour
1 egg yolk, beaten
1 teaspoon minced parsley
⅔ cup evaporated milk or thin cream

Chop the hard part of the clams, or grind them. Make a
roux of butter, flour, and liquor. (This merely means melt
butter, blend in flour, over a medium heat, stir constantly, add
liquor and keep stirring until smooth. Easy.) Add clams, milk
or cream, egg and freshly ground pepper.

Line a deep pie dish with pastry. Pour in the clams. Cover
with an upper crust and bake until the pastry is brown, about
40 minutes.

Serves 4-5.

*N.B. You may use canned minced clams, but shorten the
baking time as these are already cooked.*

LOUELLA'S CLAM PIE

Pastry to line a 9-inch pie tin

2 7½-oz. cans minced clams, drained (save liquor)
6 slices cooked bacon, crumbled
3 tablespoons minced onion cooked until golden in 2 tablespoons of the bacon drippings
4 eggs, slightly beaten
1 cup milk
1 cup clam liquor
Pepper and salt to taste

Combine eggs, milk, clam liquor, seasonings. Sprinkle
bacon over pastry shell. Add diced clams. Pour the egg mixture over. Bake in a moderate hot oven (375°) for 40 minutes,
or until a knife inserted in the center comes out clean.

Serves 4-6.

CRAB CASSEROLE

 1 package chopped frozen spinach
 1 cup grated Cheddar cheese
 1 can crab meat (large size)
 1 tablespoon lemon juice
 1 small onion, minced
 1 6-oz. can tomato paste
 ½ pint sour cream
 Salt, pepper, paprika
 1 tablespoon dry sherry

Cook the spinach as directed. Fork it lightly into a greased casserole (1-quart size). Sprinkle with half of the cheese, then place the crab meat in, and add lemon juice. Mix remaining ingredients and pour over the casserole. Add remaining cheese.

Bake in a moderate oven (350°) for 35 minutes.

Serves 4.

N.B. This is almost a version of Chicken Divan. We like to use half sharp cheese and half Parmesan, grated.

HOT CRABMEAT SANDWICH

1 6½-oz. can crabmeat
Mayonnaise
4 slices white bread, toasted on one side
4 slices Swiss or American cheese
4 slices tomatoes
4 strips bacon, cut in half
Dry mustard

Remove any shells from crabmeat, and add enough mayonnaise to make the mixture spread easily. Spread crab mixture on 4 slices bread, on untoasted side. Cover each slice with cheese, top with tomato, sprinkle lightly with dry mustard, arrange bacon on top.

Broil until bacon is crisp and cheese melts.

Serves 4.

LOBSTER NEWBURG

2 cups boiled diced lobster meat, or two 6½-oz. cans
1 cup light cream
2 egg yolks, beaten
1 tablespoon flour
¼ teaspoon salt
4 tablespoons melted butter
1 teaspoon lemon juice
Paprika to taste

Heat lobster in 3 tablespoons of melted butter. Do not let butter brown. In another saucepan stir flour into one tablespoon of melted butter, add cream and heat, stirring until smooth. Remove from fire as it begins to boil, add beaten egg yolks and stir until mixture thickens.

Add lobster and seasonings.

Serve at once on thin dry toast or crisp crackers.

Serves 4.

N.B. This is a variation of the usual sherry in Newburg, and is more delicate. The lemon juice does not mask the taste of the lobster.

LOBSTER STEW—THE NEW ENGLAND WAY

2 lobsters (at least 1 pound each)
½ cup butter or margarine
1½ quarts light cream (top milk will do, if necessary)
2 tablespoons or more sherry
Seasoning to taste

Boil the lobsters fifteen minutes (in sea water if you can get it). Remove to a dripping pan and, when cool enough, split open and remove the meat. Do not skip the coral and tomalley (red roe and green liver). Press the juice from the feelers. Put the lobster meat, tomalley, roe, and juice from the dripping pan in a pan with the melted butter or margarine, and stir constantly until the butter or margarine covers everything except your apron. Cover and let stand several hours. Then heat the cream in a double boiler until it is hot but not boiling, add lobster meat and juice and seasonings. Watch the salt if you have used sea water.

Let cool. Then put in the refrigerator for 24 hours.

Reheat, check the seasoning, and add the sherry.

Serves six.

N.B. Lobster stew, like Clam Chowder, needs to mellow. Or, as we say in my part of the country, it has to ripen.

Serve this in a big tureen, preferably ironstone, for the creamy color is just right with the pink-rose of the stew. Add crusty French or Italian bread, a green salad and plenty of hot coffee. Nobody will want dessert. You may offer them fresh fruit, crisp crackers and Camembert cheese, if you must. But don't use a strong cheese, this is no time for the robust Cheddar after the rich savory lobster!

SCALLOPED OYSTERS

1 quart oysters
½ cup butter or margarine
½ cup flour
1½ teaspoons paprika
½ teaspoon salt
¼ teaspoon black pepper
Dash Cayenne
1 onion, finely minced
½ green pepper, chopped or minced
½ bud garlic, crushed
1 teaspoon lemon juice
1 tablespoon Worcestershire
¼ cup cracker crumbs

Melt butter or margarine, add flour, and cook until light brown—about 5 minutes. Stir constantly. Add paprika, salt, pepper, cayenne and cook 3 minutes more. Add onion, green pepper, garlic and simmer 5 minutes. Remove from fire and add lemon juice, Worcestershire.

Meanwhile heat oysters in their own liquor until edges curl. Add oysters to the first mixture and pour into a baking dish. Sprinkle crumbs over top and bake in a hot oven (400°) for about 30 minutes.

Serves 4-6.

N.B. I first ate this dish in Williamsburg and begged the recipe from Travis House as it was the best I ever tasted.

SHRIMP AMANDINE

2 pounds shrimp, fresh or frozen, cooked
¾ cup raw rice
2 tablespoons butter or margarine
¼ cup chopped green pepper
½ cup chopped onion
Salt to taste, pepper to taste
1 can condensed tomato soup
1 cup cream
½ cup sherry, dry
½ cup sliced blanched almonds

Cook the rice as the package directs, drain, and let cool. Meanwhile, sauté the onion and green pepper in butter or margarine about five or six minutes. Then add seasonings, the soup, cream and sherry and almonds. Reserve a few whole shrimps for garnish and mix the rest with the rice and sauce. Turn into a 2-quart casserole, greased, and bake about 30 minutes in a moderate oven. Add the whole shrimps, chopped parsley, paprika, and a few more almonds, and bake about 10 minutes longer.

A sprinkle of Parmesan does no harm.

Garnish with celery tips, watercress or more parsley.

Serves 6 very well, more if you have enough side dishes.

GRILLED MARINATED SHRIMP

2 pounds shrimp
Marinade:
    3 cloves garlic, crushed
    ⅔ cup minced onion
    ¼ cup chopped parsley
    1 teaspoon dried basil
    1 teaspoon dry mustard
    1 teaspoon salt
    ½ cup olive oil
    2 tablespoons lemon juice

Mix the marinade ingredients well. Split the shrimp down the back. Remove veins, leaving the shell on. Cut into the flesh about halfway. Place them in a bowl and pour the marinade over. Marinate at least 2 hours, then pour all into a broiling pan. Broil about 3 inches from the heat, turning frequently until the shrimp are pink, the shells browned slightly and curled back.

Serves 4-6.

CREOLE SHRIMP

1 pound fresh or frozen shrimp, cooked
¼ cup butter or margarine
1 large onion, minced
1 cup green pepper, chopped
1 clove garlic
2 teaspoons flour
2 cups canned tomatoes
1½ teaspoons salt
Dash of rosemary
Paprika and pepper to taste

Melt butter or margarine and sauté onion, pepper, garlic for 10 minutes. Then stir in flour, and when blended add tomatoes and seasonings and bring to boiling point. Cover, reduce the heat, and simmer for about 15 minutes. Then add the shrimp and reheat, but do not boil.

Serve on fluffy rice.

Serves 4-5.

SEAFOOD CASSEROLE

1 can (½ pound) lobster, shrimp, or salmon
1 box frozen peas, thawed
1 can condensed celery soup
1¼ cups milk
Salt, pepper, paprika
1 tablespoon lemon juice, fresh or canned
1⅓ cups cooked rice
Parmesan cheese, grated

Cook soup, milk, seasonings, stirring until well blended. In a greased 1½-quart casserole, pour half of the soup. Then add alternate layers of seafood, rice, peas. Add the remaining soup. Sprinkle the cheese over the top. Bake, covered, in a moderate oven until bubbly (20 minutes).

Serves 4.

N.B. This may be varied endlessly. You may use a mixture of tuna, salmon, crab, lobster. You may add diced onion and green pepper, sautéed in butter or margarine. You may like to add a dash of sherry. You may garnish with freshly chopped parsley and slivers of pimento. You may use cream of mushroom soup if you prefer.

Meats

I WAS BROUGHT UP to believe that there was scarcely an ailment that would not be cured by a steak, or a slice of rosy rare roast beef, or a couple of broiled lamb chops. I still find, after a hard day, that the very smell of a rib roast browning in the oven gives a "lift to my forehead," as a Southern friend used to say.

I like to think of the poet Shelley who was advised to eat "A couple of mutton chops, well-peppered" when he was ill, and he recovered rapidly from his diet of nuts and fruit.

The expensive cuts of meat have been a luxury most of the time since I grew up, but the cheaper cuts, properly cooked, can make a gourmet dinner. The meat we buy today is better in quality, on the whole, because we have learned so much about the science of agriculture. We may now get it canned or frozen, not to mention dehydrated in soups and gravies.

We also have a new substance called "meat tenderizer" which can be sprinkled on any not-too-tender piece of meat, according to the directions on the bottle. This, plus proper cooking, can make a round steak really fork-tender. In the meat recipes that follow, use the tenderizer whenever you use any less-expensive cut of meat.

A word on timing meats. A meat thermometer is a great help. Timing charts are in practically all general cookbooks. And practically all of them, for my money, call for too much time. For a rare roast beef, I take it from the oven the minute the mercury gets in sight, which is below the rare mark. I cut the time on lamb about a third. I think the even heat of modern insulated ovens cooks far faster than the time charts allow for. Also roasts keep on cooking about 15 minutes after you take them from the oven, cooking themselves from their own heat.

BEEF BURGUNDY

2 pounds beef stew meat, cubed
Flour
3 tablespoons bacon fat or shortening
½ cup diced onion
1 cup diced celery
1 cup diced carrots
1 can condensed consommé
1 cup water
½ cup burgundy wine
Salt and pepper to taste

Dredge meat with flour, brown slowly in the fat. Add remaining ingredients, cover and simmer gently until meat is tender, about 1½ hours. Stir often, adding a little water if needed.
Serves 5-6.

GLAMOR VERSION BEEF BURGUNDY

Use top round or round steak for the beef. Use leeks, carrots, onions, chopped parsley, chives, 1 crushed clove garlic, and brown separately.

Brown cubed and floured beef in a braising kettle. Light 2 tablespoons brandy in a ladle and pour over the beef, burning. Add vegetable mixture, and a *bouquet garni* of 2 whole cloves, 8 crushed peppercorns, pinch marjoram, salt. Pour over burgundy to cover, cover tightly, bake in a moderate oven (350°) for 3 hours.

Discard bouquet, transfer meat to hot platter, heat sauce to boiling point and pour over the meat.

EVA'S FOIL-BAKED BEEF

4 minute steaks, frozen, per person
2 slices sweet onion per person
½ peeled sliced potato per person
Salt, pepper, butter or margarine

Cut 2 pieces of aluminum foil per serving (½ again as large as the steaks). Lay the first 2 steaks on the bottom piece of aluminum foil, then the onion, seasonings, then the potato slices. Season, add the butter or margarine. Top with the remaining steaks. Now lay the second piece of foil on top, bring the edges of the bottom piece up and fold over snugly, sealing by pressing well with your fingers. Bake in a moderate oven (350°) for 50 minutes.

N.B. You may vary this by adding a slice of fresh tomato or some chopped green pepper on top of the upper steaks.

This may be cooked on a picnic grill. Turn once, and allow an hour. Add crusty French bread and a tossed salad. For a picnic, just remove the top foil, unfold the edges of the bottom piece and slide a paper plate under for support.

BEEFSTEAK AND KIDNEY PIE

2 pounds beef chuck, cut in 1-inch cubes
1 pound lamb kidneys, cut in pieces and with membrane removed
1 cube beef suet (1½ inch)
1 medium onion, sliced
1 teaspoon Worcestershire
1 can bouillon
Pastry

Chop the suet, and cook slowly in a skillet until the fat is tried out (melted). You need 5 or 6 tablespoons fat. Sauté the onion slices in half of the fat in a heavy kettle. When the onion is golden, but not brown, remove and reserve, and sauté the beef and kidneys in the same kettle, adding more fat as needed. When the meat is brown, add the onion, Worcestershire and bouillon, and simmer, covered, until tender. This takes about an hour.

Now remove the meat and onion slices with a slotted spoon and keep warm. Put 1½ tablespoons flour and ½ cup water in a covered jar and shake well. Stir this slowly into the kettle, stirring until the gravy is thickened. Add the meat and onions to the gravy and place in a deep casserole (or in 4 individual casseroles if you wish). Cover with pastry. Bake in a hot oven (425°) until the pastry is golden brown (about 20 minutes).

Serves 4.

N.B. You may prepare the beef and kidney part ahead of time, in fact, it improves with resting. Then add your pastry and bake while your guests nibble appetizers.

LONDON BROIL

1 flank steak
Butter or margarine

Pre-heat your broiler until it is sizzling hot. Place the steak on the broiler rack and broil about 3 inches from the heat, 3 minutes to a side. (If you like it well done, add 1 minute for each side, but be careful.)

Lift the steak out and with a sharp knife, carve it in thin strips diagonally across the grain. This will be crosswise of your piece.

Serve on a warm platter, with a little butter or margarine over it.

N.B. The flavor of flank steak is one of the best. But because it has long-grain fibres, many people avoid it. (See FLANK STEAK BRAISED WITH VEGETABLES.)

With London Broil, scalloped potatoes, fresh or frozen asparagus, coffee, and a fruit bowl add up to happy dining.

BAKED CORNED-BEEF HASH

2 cans corned beef
⅔ cup top milk
Pinch dry mustard

Mix the corned beef and milk and turn into a greased casserole, adding the mustard.

Put in medium oven (350°) and, when the milk is hot, stir it all with a fork once. Bake until bubbly (20-25 minutes).
Serves 4.

N.B. Could hardly be easier and tastes delicious. Takes about 2 minutes to pop it in the oven, while those unexpected guests divest themselves of hats and coats, and you mix the green salad while they sip their tomato juice or cocktails.

If they phone from the postoffice that they are coming, you may also serve them cornsticks, made of cornbread mix and baked with the hash. Or corn muffins if you have no cornstick iron pans.

Put the catsup or chili sauce or Sauce Diable on the table.

Break out the spiced peaches for dessert and keep the coffee hot.

STILLMEADOW HAMBURGER BAKE

Amounts vary according to how many hungry people have descended on you:—

Hamburger
Prepared mustard, salt, pepper
Onion, sliced thin
Tomatoes

Pat hamburger (ground round steak if possible) into a round cake tin. Spread with prepared mustard, sprinkle with salt and pepper. Lay thin slices of onion over it, covering the meat well.

Then lay slices of tomatoes over the onion, and do not spare the horses on the tomatoes. Lay sliced green pepper over the tomatoes.

Put another layer of the beef on top for a lid, and top that with several slices of tomato.

Bake in a moderate (350°) oven until the hamburger is done. It takes about half an hour, depending, of course, on how thick your layers are. The onion and tomato will cook into the meat and the juices blend.

If you use regular hamburger, which has fat added, be sure your pan is deep.

Serve with fluffy baked potatoes, or if you haven't time for them, noodles or instant rice. Potatoes, by the way, bake in half the time if you slice them lengthwise, serrate them with a sharp knife—which means make cuts crosswise and lengthwise, but not very deep—and spread shortening on the cut surface.

HUNGARIAN STEAK

1½ pounds round steak, cubed
¼ cup chopped green pepper
½ cup chopped onion
1 No. 2 can tomatoes
Salt and pepper

Dredge steak in flour and brown in butter or margarine or fat. Arrange in layers in a frying pan, with the tomatoes, pepper and onion between the layers and on top. Cover and simmer slowly for 1½ hours.

Add salt and pepper the last twenty minutes.

Serves 4-6.

Serve with fluffy baked potatoes and a green salad.

BURTON'S SAVORY MEAT LOAF

2 pounds beef chuck or round steak ground with a good chunk of suet (approximately ½ cup), cut fine
2 cups bread crumbs or prepared dressing
2 eggs, beaten

Into beaten eggs mix:

2 tablespoons prepared mustard
3 tablespoons horseradish
2 teaspoons salt
Pepper to taste
½ cup catsup
1 large onion, minced
1 crushed clove garlic

Mix suet with meat and crumbs and knead well. Turn into a greased loaf pan and bake in a moderate oven (325°) about an hour or until well browned on top.

Pour off surplus fat and save it for soups or gravies.

N.B. Wonderful sliced cold, as it keeps its shape better than most loaves.

LOUELLA'S SWEDISH MEATBALLS IN SOUR-CREAM SAUCE

1½ pounds ground beef
2 cups bread cubes soaked in milk (½ cup is right)
1 chopped medium onion
3 beaten eggs
2½ teaspoons salt
¼ teaspoon pepper
2 teaspoons ground nutmeg
2 teaspoons paprika
1 teaspoon dry mustard
1 teaspoon dried mixed herbs
¼ cup butter or margarine

Squeeze bread cubes dry, and add to the beef. Sauté the onion in 2 tablespoons butter or margarine, then add eggs and seasonings, and mix well with the beef.

Form into small balls (the size of a large walnut). Makes about 72 meatballs. Brown in a skillet with ¼ cup butter or margarine, turning to brown evenly on all sides. Keep warm in the oven while you make the sauce.

SAUCE:

Add flour to the drippings in the skillet, using 1 tablespoon flour per tablespoon of fat. Add 2 teaspoons beef concentrate. Stir over low heat until thickened, then add 1 cup commercial sour cream. Re-heat but do not boil or the cream will curdle. Pour over the meatballs and serve at once.

Serves 4-6.

Serve with noodles, a mixed vegetable salad, coffee.

FLANK STEAK BRAISED WITH VEGETABLES

1½ pounds flank steak
2 tablespoons flour and 1 teaspon salt for dredging
Butter or margarine
1½ cups raw sliced potatoes
½ cup sliced onions
1 green pepper, sliced
1 cup canned tomatoes (or an equal amount of fresh stewed
    tomatoes)

Have your butcher, if he is your friend, make shallow cuts on the flank steak. If he does not like you, do it yourself cutting across the grain with a sharp knife.

Dredge on both sides with the flour and salt, dot with butter or margarine and place in a rectangular baking pan. Cover with the potatoes, then with onions, and tomatoes.

Cover tightly and cook in a slow oven for 2 hours or until tender. Add tomato juice if it seems dry.

Lift onto a hot platter carefully, to preserve the layers of vegetables, and serve at once.

Serves 4-6.

N.B. You can add mushrooms, fresh or canned, if company comes. The tomato tenderizes the meat and the flavor of a properly done flank steak is second to none, not even Porterhouse. You may add MSG and garlic salt and a whiff of parsley flakes. But, as they say, good wine needs no bush, and this needs no extras to taste good!

POT ROAST SPECIAL

1 pot roast (or 3-4 lbs. short ribs)
2 tablespoons hot prepared mustard
½ teaspoon salt
½ teaspoon black pepper
½ teaspoon chili powder
1 crushed clove garlic
5 tablespoons olive oil
½ cup burgundy

Marinate the pot roast or ribs in the rest of the ingredients (blend them together first) for 6-12 hours.

Heat 2 tablespoons olive oil in heavy kettle. Brown meat. Add the marinade and ½ cup water. Cover closely and simmer until tender.

RIB ROAST OF BEEF WITH YORKSHIRE PUDDING

1 Rib roast—4-6 lbs.

Wipe the meat with a damp cloth. Season with salt and pepper and mixed herbs, and dried parsley. Tuck very fine slivers of garlic in several places under the fat, and work in a few celery leaves.

Roast uncovered in a slow oven (300°-350°), allowing 18 minutes a pound. If you have a meat thermometer insert it carefully in the center of the meat.

Now, take the roast out *before* the thermometer registers rare beef. For one thing, a roast will go on cooking fifteen minutes after you take it out. For another, the thermometer at rare gives you a medium-well-done roast. Maybe you like that, if so it is a pity.

Half an hour before the roast is done, make the Yorkshire pudding. This is my Aunt Minnie's recipe and is the best, I believe.

YORKSHIRE PUDDING:

1 cup flour sifted with 1 teaspoon salt
3 well-beaten eggs
2 cups milk

Mix the eggs and milk, add to the flour and beat well (rotary beater or, better still, your mixer).

Now pour off the drippings from the roasting pan, leaving about ¼ cup. Set the roast aside in a warm place, and pour the batter in the pan. Increase oven to 400° or hot, and bake 30 minutes or until it draws away from the edges and begins to be golden brown on top.

Serves 4-6.

CHINESE PEPPER STEAK

1 lb. round or flank steak cut in strips ⅛ inch thick
Salt, pepper, paprika
2 tablespoons salad oil
1 medium onion, chopped
1 clove garlic, minced
2 green peppers, diced
1 cup bouillon
1 cup drained canned tomatoes
1½ tablespoons cornstarch
2 teaspoons soy sauce
¼ cup water

Sprinkle the meat slices with salt, pepper, paprika and sauté in the oil in a large heavy skillet with onion and garlic. Add peppers when steak is browned, pour the bouillon over and simmer, covered, for about 10 minutes. Then add the tomatoes and simmer 5 more minutes.

Meanwhile mix the cornstarch, soy sauce and water together, add to the meat mixture and stir until the sauce is thick and clear (a few minutes will do it).

Serves 4.

N.B. If you use flank steak, cut across the grain, not with it. Delicious!
Serve with hot, fluffy rice, plenty of coffee, or tea.

SUKIYAKI

- 1½ pounds round steak (fairly thick)
- 4 small white onions
- 2 bunches scallions or young leeks
- 2 green peppers, medium size
- 1 head celery (discard outer stalks)
- 1 can sliced mushrooms (medium size)
- 1 pound spinach
- 2 tablespoons butter, margarine, or drippings

Slice the meat into thin bite-sized pieces, using a sharp knife. Cut across the grain and keep the slices ⅛ inch thick. Cut the onions into 8ths, slice the scallions or leeks lengthwise, then crosswise into small pieces. Seed the peppers and slice thinly lengthwise. Cut the celery in small bits. Shred the spinach (washed and crisped).

The Sauce:

- ½ cup soy sauce
- 1 bouillon cube dissolved in ½ cup boiling water
- 1 tablespoon sugar
- Salt to taste

Blend the sauce ingredients.

Melt the fat in a heavy skillet or in an electric frying pan, add half of the meat, and stir until browned evenly. Then add half the onions, peppers and celery, then half the sauce. Stir lightly. Cook over medium heat about 5 minutes. Then stir in half the scallions and the mushrooms (drained). Cook 1 minute. Add half the spinach and cook 1 minute.

Serve with hot fluffy rice.

Serves 4.

Repeat the process for the second helpings.

N.B. This is pre-eminently a table-cooked dish, but if you have no electric frying pan, you may do it in an iron or heavy

106

aluminum skillet. For a buffet, the table may be set with bowls of the chopped vegetables and meat and sauce, and guests can help with the cooking, which is brief enough so they won't get bored!

This is not a traditional Sukiyaki, which calls for bamboo shoots, bean curd and so on. But it tastes delicious, is easy, and inexpensive.

The quick-cooking keeps the vegetables crisp, and the second helping cooks while guests consume the first. You may, also, do the chopping and slicing ahead of time, keeping the ingredients crisp in their own bowls covered with aluminum foil or waxed paper.

If you have no table-warmer to keep the rice hot, use a heavy casserole dipped in very hot water. Put the rice in, and run it in the oven for a few minutes.

TERIYAKI

Sirloin steak, cut in 2-inch cubes
¾ cup soy sauce
⅓ cup dry sherry
1 clove garlic, crushed

Marinate the steak cubes in the soy sauce, sherry and garlic for at least an hour. Thread the cubes on skewers and broil, preferably on a charcoal grill in the back yard.

N.B. Count on 4 to 5 cubes per person, or at least 3 for delicate guests. If the budget is bent, try round steak, and tenderize it with a meat tenderizer, according to directions on the bottle.

While the steak is marinating, cook individual packages of sliced potatoes, sliced onion, seasoned with butter or margarine, salt, freshly ground pepper, on the grill. Use aluminum foil, and be sure you double wrap those edges. Cut two squares of foil for each serving, put the vegetables in the center of one, fold the bottom layer over the top and turn the edges tightly together. Allow about 40 minutes on the grill.

Make the coffee in the house; there isn't room for it.

NEW ENGLAND BOILED DINNER

6 pound cut of corned beef, brisket or rump

Place in cold water to cover, add ½ clove garlic and 6 peppercorns.

Bring to boiling and cook slowly, skimming when needed. It takes about 4 hours as a rule. Test for tenderness with a fork. When it is tender, remove it and add to the stock the following:

6 carrots
3 large yellow turnips, cut in halves or quarters
4 small parsnips
8 small peeled onions

Simmer 15 minutes, then add 6 medium potatoes, peeled and cut in quarters, and a head of cabbage cut in quarters.

When the vegetables are tender, return the corned beef to the pot and reheat.

Serve on a hot platter, garnished with parsley.

Serves 6-8.

N.B. Gild the lily, if you want it gilded, with horseradish sauce. (Beat sour cream with fresh grated horseradish or prepared bottle horseradish. If you use the prepared, add a little lemon juice.)

No doubt it was the New England boiled dinner that gave the early folk energy to fell trees, conquer the wilderness. It has been around a long time, possibly it stems from the English boiled mutton. It still warms the cockles of the heart on a snowy winter night.

QUICK BOILED DINNER

1 12-ounce can corned beef, sliced
4 small potatoes, scrubbed
6 scallions
2 or 3 carrots, scrubbed and quartered
½ head young green cabbage, cut in quarters

Cook potatoes and carrots in boiling salted water until half tender—about 10 minutes. Then lay the cabbage quarters over the potatoes and carrots, next the scallions, and finally the corned beef. Cover and steam until the cabbage is tender. The beef, scallions and cabbage should not be down in the liquor but on top of the potatoes and carrots. Drain and serve on a warm platter, dressed with salt, pepper and melted butter or margarine.

Serves 2.

For a sauce for the corned beef slices, use Western View Mustard Sauce, or combine 2 parts commercial sour cream with 1 part preserved mustard.

N.B. I learned this from Louella Shouer, whose Quick and Easy Meals for Two *has been a classic for some time. The recipe has been popular enough to be copied in another publication, so here goes again. I especially like it in hot weather after cold dishes begin to pall, for it is a rib-sticking dish but does not heat up the kitchen as a regular boiled dinner does.*

LOIS KLAKRING'S CHICKEN AND HAM CASEROLE

6 equal slices each of cooked chicken and ham
1 onion, minced
½ cup sliced mushrooms
Paprika, salt
¾ cup hot cream
Grated Parmesan cheese
Butter or margarine

Cook onion in butter or margarine until golden, add mushrooms, paprika and salt. (If you have no fresh mushrooms, substitute canned, drained.) Simmer 5 minutes for fresh mushrooms, 2 for canned.

Turn mixture into a greased casserole, put in ham, then chicken on ham, then pour the hot cream over, and sprinkle with the cheese. Bake in a hot oven (400°) until bubbly and brown.

Serves 4-6.

N.B. If you use an oblong flattish casserole, you will have an easier time serving.

111

SMILEY BURNETTE'S SPICED LEG OF LAMB

1 leg of lamb
1 onion, sliced thin
1 tablespoon salt
1 tablespoon whole pepper
1 tablespoon allspice
⅛ pound butter or margarine
2 bay leaves
1 cup water
½ cup cider vinegar
1 pint plum jam
Flour
1 cup port wine

Crush the salt, pepper, allspice in a mortar or in a cloth. Roll the onion slices in the powder, make incisions in the lamb and insert the slices. Put the roast in the roaster with bay leaves, butter, and water, and sprinkle any powder left over the top. Roast 1 hour, covered. Then add the vinegar and spread the plum jam over the meat. Finish roasting uncovered, basting every 10 minutes or so, until the meat is tender when pierced with a fork. Remove to a heated platter and make the gravy.

GRAVY:

Add flour to the drippings in the pan, using 2 tablespoons flour to 2 tablespoons drippings. Add the wine, stirring constantly. When the gravy is thickened, strain, and serve with the roast. (Or you may shake the wine and flour up in a covered jar, and add to the drippings, stirring until thickened.)

N.B. This is designed to make those who simply hate lamb pass their plates for a second helping.

I asked Smiley once how he happened to be such a superb cook.

"I got hungry," he said.

As a star of Westerns, a TV performer, showman, he is on the road going places more often than not. "But I got tired of hotel and restaurant meals," he says, "so I mostly cook my own." On the road, with his special portable kitchen packed in suitcases, his herbs, spices and staples in a carrying case, he cooks backstage, in arena dressing rooms, in hotel bedrooms (by special permission), or by the side of the road.

This spiced leg of lamb, however, he cooked at Stillmeadow, where the oven is not portable.

LAMB STEW

2 pounds shoulder or neck of lamb, cut in 2-inch cubes
1 medium onion, sliced thin
5 medium potatoes, peeled and quartered
¾ cup peas, cooked
1 cup tomato paste
1 cup meat stock
2 tablespoons butter or margarine
1 cup sour cream

Melt butter or margarine in a heavy kettle and sauté the onion in it until golden. Season with salt, freshly ground pepper, and paprika, add the lamb and let it brown, stirring with a wooden spoon to brown the pieces evenly. Remove the meat to a soup kettle. Add tomato paste and meat stock to the fat and stir well until blended, then pour this over the lamb. Bring to a boil, then lower the heat, cover, and simmer gently for an hour or so. Add the potatoes for the last 25 minutes of cooking, and check the seasoning at this time. Add the peas for the final 5 minutes. Remove the meat and vegetables with a slotted spoon and gradually add the sour cream to the gravy, but do not let it boil. Pour the gravy over, and serve at once.

Serves 4-5.

MIDSUMMER HAM BUFFET

1 canned cooked ham
1 package lemon gelatin
Parsley
Pimento strips for garnish

Remove the juices from the canned ham, and wipe it dry with a paper towel. Place it on a rack over a platter. Prepare the gelatin according to directions on the package and let it cool until it is beginning to set. Pour a layer over the ham, let cool in the refrigerator until it is firm, then pour the remaining gelatin over and chill until glazed. Just before it is jellied, add strips of pimento, and sprigs of parsley for decoration.

N.B. For easy serving for company, slice the ham when you have dried it, then tie it together with a fine string. The slices will slide neatly on the plate. Remove the string as you serve.

Since this is cold, serve one hot dish with it. I favor a casserole of baked beans, bubbly and spicy. A mixed green salad, and garlic toasted French bread, plus the coffee complete the buffet.

Honeydew melon wedges garnished with mint sprigs dipped in powdered sugar are my last word on this one. With ham, try for a dessert that will not be sweet or rich.

STILLMEADOW SAVORY HAM PIE

1½ or 2 cups cooked left-over ham, diced
4 tablespoons onion, diced
4 tablespoons green pepper, diced
4 tablespoons butter or margarine
6 tablespoons flour
1 can condensed chicken or celery or mushroom soup
1⅓ cups milk
1 tablespoon lemon juice (fresh, frozen, canned)

Cook onion and pepper in the fat until golden, stir in flour and, when it is bubbly, add milk and soup. Stir until smooth, add lemon juice and ham and put into a deep greased casserole.

Top with a crust made of the following:

1½ cups prepared biscuit mix
6 tablespoons milk
½ cup grated Cheddar cheese (or Swiss if you prefer)

Mix cheese and flour and stir in milk to form a soft dough. Roll out, or pat in shape on a floured board. Cut with a doughnut cutter. Lay on top of the ham mixture and tuck bits of pimento in the small holes left by the cutter. Bake in a hot oven (450°) until the top is crusty and brown.

Serves 4-6.

N.B. This is a rib-sticking winter-night dish. Needs a tossed green salad with a lemon juice-oil dressing, and a fruit compote for dessert. Plenty of coffee.

PORK CHOPS AND CABBAGE

6 pork chops
1 large head fresh cabbage
1 large onion
Milk
Salt, pepper, paprika

Brown the pork chops, using a little butter or margarine if necessary. Slice the onion and add to the chops after you have turned them.

Arrange the chops in a large greased baking dish or casserole with the onion slices around them. Season well.

Slice the cabbage thinly with a sharp knife and pack it tightly on the chops, filling the casserole almost to the top (it will shrink). Pour over milk enough to barely cover. Add more salt, pepper, paprika. Bake, covered, for 45-60 minutes (depends on the cabbage) in a moderate oven. Test with a fork for tenderness.

Serves 4-6.

Serve with baked potatoes, for the pork, onion, milk makes a gravy that begs for a baked potato.

N.B. You may have some of the milk and cabbage left over. And next day's luncheon soup is ready!

SAVORY PORK RING

3 cups left-over pork roast, diced finely
1½ cups cornmeal (water-ground if possible)
⅓ cup sifted flour
1½ teaspoons salt
3 teaspoons baking powder
2 eggs, beaten
1¼ cups milk
¼ cup melted butter or margarine
1½ cups gravy

Sift the dry ingredients together. Add eggs and milk to butter or margarine, and pour over the dry mixture. Stir until moistened. Bake in a greased 9-inch ring mold at 400° or hot oven about 25 minutes. Test center with a straw; if it comes out clean, the cornbread is done.

Meanwhile heat the pork and gravy. Unmold the corn ring and put it on a hot platter. Fill the center with the pork and gravy.

Serves 4.

N.B. If you are short of gravy, use cream of mushroom or chicken soup, diluted with ⅓ can of water or milk.

STILLMEADOW SPARERIBS

4 pounds spareribs cut in serving-size pieces
1 large onion, diced
½ cup drippings (see below)
½ cup catsup
1 pint tomato juice
2 teaspoons chili powder
1 tablespoon prepared mustard
¼ cup vinegar
1 teaspoon salt
¼ teaspoon pepper
2 bay leaves
1 tablespoon Worcestershire
2½ cups boiling water

Salt and pepper the ribs, dredge with flour and broil until brown. Turn once.

Drain ½ cup of the drippings from the broiler pan and put in a large skillet. Brown the onion in the drippings, add the rest of the ingredients and simmer 5 minutes.

Place the ribs in a large casserole or baking pan, pour the sauce over, cover (use aluminum foil if your pan has no cover) and bake 1½ hours.

Serves 4.

N.B. This is one of the top buffet-dinner dishes. Can be made the day before and reheated. Serve with crusty French bread and a green salad.

COLD TONGUE CURRY

1 cup cooked beef tongue, sliced thin (or one 7½-oz. can
    of tongue)
3 hard-cooked eggs, sliced
1 envelope unflavored gelatin
1 cup cold water
1 can cream of mushroom soup
1¼ teaspoon curry powder
1 teaspoon lemon juice
Salt, paprika
Green pepper rings, sliced stuffed olives for garnish

Stir the curry into ½ cup of the water, then sprinkle the
gelatin over the top. After 5 minutes dissolve over boiling
water.

Combine remaining ½ cup water with the soup, lemon
juice, seasonings. Stir in the gelatin. Let cool until beginning
to set. Then pour a layer of the gelatin in a mold or flat baking dish (such as you use for au gratin recipes). Arrange the
sliced eggs on the gelatin. Set in the refrigerator a few minutes, then arrange the sliced tongue for the second layer,
pour over the remaining gelatin and set until firm. Unmold
at serving time, and garnish with pepper rings and olives.

Serves 4-6.

*N.B. A side bowl of mayonnaise with 1 teaspoon of mus-
tard added makes a fine complement.*

*For a company one-dish dinner, arrange sliced fresh to-
matoes and cucumbers around the curry.*

BRAISED SWEETBREADS

3 pair sweetbreads
Juice of ½ lemon
3 tablespoons butter or margarine
1 onion, chopped
1 carrot, diced
1 bay leaf
2 sprigs parsley
½ cup dry white table wine
1 cup chicken broth (fresh or made with a cube or canned)

Soak the sweetbreads in ice water for about an hour, then plunge them in salted boiling water to which lemon juice has been added. Cook 15 minutes, remove, run cold water over at once. When cool, discard the tough membranes.

In an oven casserole, on a spreader, melt the butter or margarine, add the vegetables and seasonings and cook until the carrots turn golden. Sprinkle a little flour over them, add the sweetbreads, wine and chicken broth. Bring to a boil, then cover the casserole and put in a moderate oven (350°) for about half an hour. Turn them once or twice and test with a fork for tenderness.

Remove the sweetbreads to a hot platter, strain the juices and add a tablespoon or two of sherry if desired.

Reheat the sauce just until it is good and hot, and pour over. **Serves 3-5 according to how you like sweetbreads.**

N.B. Most sweetbreads are overcooked. If they are young and tender, they need not be parboiled as long.

TAMALE PARTY PIE

2 pounds ground lean beef or pork
2 large onions, diced
Salt and pepper to taste
1½ cups cornmeal
1½ cups milk
1 No. 2½ can tomatoes
1 can cream-style corn (15½ oz. or 1 lb.)
1 can (8½ oz.) ripe olives, sliced
2 tablespoons chili powder
1½ teaspoons salt

Brown the meat and onions, adding fat if the meat is really lean. Add salt and pepper. Simmer 40 minutes, stirring occasionally.

Meanwhile mix cornmeal, milk and salt in a big kettle. Add tomatoes and cook slowly about 30 minutes, stirring often. Then add corn, olives, chili powder and mix well.

Combine meat and cornmeal mixture and place in a greased casserole or baking dish. Bake at 300° for 1½ hours or until it begins to draw away from the sides of the pan.

This amount makes 12 portions.

N.B. You may make this the day before and reheat. And greet the guests with a smile.

TACOS

Left-over roast lamb (a cup or more)
1 can enchilada sauce
1 head lettuce
1 medium onion, chopped
1 can tortillas (or fresh if you can get them)

Grind the lettuce in a food chopper or chop finely in a wooden bowl, having 3 or 4 cups shredded.

Grind the meat. Mix lettuce and meat and season well with salt and pepper. Add chopped onions and enchilada sauce—just enough to moisten.

Fold tortillas in half and fry lightly in a skillet with hot fat. Turn once. Take out and put the filling in each tortilla, folding the tortilla back to keep the filling in.

Drop in deep hot fat again, just long enough to heat.

If the remaining sauce is not enough to spoon over, add a can of tomato paste or some canned tomatoes, reheat and serve.

Serves 3-4.

VERA WILKINS' VEAL CASSEROLE

2 cups left-over roast veal, sliced
1 cup chopped celery
½ chopped green onions or scallions, tops and all
¼ cup chopped green pepper
1 can condensed cream of chicken soup
½ cup milk
1 can Chow Mein noodles
1 4-oz. can button mushrooms
1 teaspoon soy sauce
½ teaspoon steak sauce or Worcestershire

Mix together the veal, celery, onions, green pepper. Add the milk to the chicken soup, then add to the meat mixture. Add all but ¼ can of the noodles, and the mushrooms, soy sauce, steak sauce. Taste for seasoning, add salt and pepper if needed.

Put the mixture in a greased casserole, top with the extra noodles and bake in a moderate oven (350°) until bubbly.

Serves 4-5.

N.B. Serve with orange and onion salad or a tossed green salad, coffee and, for dessert, nothing heavier than a custard.

VEAL CUTLET VIENNESE

2 pounds veal cutlet, cut in serving pieces
1 or 2 eggs, beaten
Flour and breadcrumbs (1 part flour to 3 of crumbs)
Butter or margarine
1 lemon, sliced thin
Salt, paprika

Pound the cutlets until very thin, using a wooden mallet or the edge of a dinner plate. Dip into the egg, and then into the flour and crumbs. Season well with salt and paprika. Let stand about half an hour for the breading to settle comfortably to the meat. Then in a heavy skillet melt the butter or margarine and sauté the cutlets over a medium heat until golden (it takes only a few minutes for each side). Remove to a hot platter and lay a slice of lemon on each cutlet. Serve at once.

Serves 4.

N.B. When my Viennese friend first made this at Still-meadow, I inquired as to what he needed for the gravy. "Gravy!" he shouted, "a sacrilege, have you NO lemons?" We had lemons. He was quite right, for the veal is so delicate that a gravy would mask the flavor. But you may always serve a casserole of macaroni and cheese as a side dish, plus a tossed salad with a little sour cream added to the basic French dressing. Comes out all right.

ROAST VEAL

1 leg of veal
Salad oil
Lemon juice
Celery, parsley, onion, garlic salt
Juniper berries, if you can get them.

Marinate the veal overnight in the salad oil and lemon juice (1 part lemon to 2 parts oil). In the morning, drain the marinade off, but do not toss it out. Make small incisions in the veal with a sharp knife and tuck in each incision a small bouquet, as it were, of celery leaves, parsley, onion slivers sprinkled with the garlic salt.

Roast, uncovered, in a slow (325°) oven. Add the juniper berries to the marinade and baste with this from time to time. The roast is done when the meat thermometer calls it just above rare, or when a two-pronged fork pierces it and the juice runs out barely pink.

Now you may throw out the marinade, and if you wish gravy keep the roast hot while you add butter or margarine to the roaster, stir in flour (2 tablespoons flour to 2 tablespoons fat.) You won't have any real drippings, so add chicken bouillon to the roux, stirring constantly.

Spike the gravy with a bit of liquid gravy maker.

N.B. Veal is very happy with asparagus, new peas, spinach. And baked potatoes. Try Floating Island pudding, which is also delicate, for the dessert, but keep the coffee hot.

Fowl

IN MY CHILDHOOD, chicken was a Sunday treat. Broilers and fried young chickens were for birthdays and holidays. The rich, rolling Wisconsin farmland supported plenty of chickens, but they were for eggs. Usually only retired fowls came to the pot. Why eat up something that could lay something that could sell? The farmers were practical. If you ate up a tender young chicken, you lost all the potential eggs.

Meat was different, for young calves were butchered unless they would be good milkers or good breeding stock. There was plenty of meat. The butchers gave away calves' liver, kidneys were for cats (except for cooks like my mother who knew their delicacy). Steak was around twenty-five cents a pound, as I remember, and you could have all the marrow bones, neck bones, shoulder bones you could carry for nothing. It was before the wars. A time of innocence and prosperity and security.

But chicken was a luxury. And then, when I moved to Virginia, we could, and did, eat chicken three times a day. The country people simply raised chickens to the broiler stage and that was that. Chicken and country cured hams and country sausage (oh, the sausage in earthenware bowls covered with a clean cloth!). I never, once, got tired of chicken. And I never have. Chicken is so versatile, it lends itself to being broiled and served on hot buttered toast for a Sunday breakfast, or to snuggling into a pastry shell with mushrooms and cream sauce for lunch, or to being cooked with sauces, Russian, Italian, and with or without noodles, with or without rice.

And what is better than a midnight piece of cold chicken well sprinkled with freshly ground pepper?

CHICKEN BORLANDIA

    1 fowl, cut up
    Baby onions (allow two or three per serving)
    Baby carrots (the same as onions)
    2 cans mushrooms (or one large can)
    Parsley
    Milk to half-cover the fowl
    Shortening

Dredge the fowl in flour, salt, pepper, paprika in a paper bag. Sauté in the shortening until golden brown. Remove, place in a greased casserole. Add milk to half-cover the chicken. Bake in a moderate oven (350°). When the chicken browns, turn it, and add carrots, onions and mushrooms (drained).

Continue baking until the chicken is tender (test with a fork).

Sprinkle chopped parsley on top, and serve in the casserole.
Serves 4-6, depending on the size of the fowl.
Serve with a salad and crunchy bread.

N.B. *"And there you are, or should be," says Barbara Borland. As a writer, gardener, housekeeper, hostess, and hiking companion for her husband, Hal, she chooses easy-to-fix dishes. This freezes well, or can be made the day before.*

127

BRUNSWICK STEW

1 5-pound stewing chicken, cut in pieces
¼ pound salt pork, diced (or bacon)
Salt, pepper
1 medium onion, diced
2 cups canned tomatoes (or four or five fresh, cut up)
2½ cups green lima beans, fresh or frozen
2½ cups canned or fresh corn kernels
3 potatoes, sliced thin
¼ pound butter
Flour

Brown the chicken in the pork drippings, add a quart of water and simmer, covered, until the chicken is tender. (If you use your pressure cooker, follow directions for fricasseeing.) When chicken is tender, cool it enough to remove meat from the bones and cut in bite-size pieces. Return to the kettle, add all the ingredients except corn and butter and flour. Cook until the vegetables are tender, then add corn and butter and cook about 5 minutes. Meanwhile blend about 4 tablespoons of flour with enough cold water to make a smooth mixture, and add to the stew to thicken it.

Serves 8.

N.B. I first had a variation of Brunswick Stew in Virginia and asked my hostess how it was made. "We just toss in whatever we have," she said vaguely. Some cooks add a can of condensed tomato soup; some, of course, add rabbit. It is company fare, served with a salad and hot biscuits.

FAY'S BAKED BROILERS

Broilers, split, ½ to each person
Rice, cooked (¾ cup per person)
Butter or margarine
Salt, paprika, pepper, onion or garlic salt

Grease an oblong dish, or a roaster if you are having a party. Lay the cooked rice, seasoned, in a mound in the center. Lay the split broilers over the rice, skin side up. Dot well with butter or margarine, and bake in a slow oven (325°) until broilers are done. Turn once during baking and add a little more butter or margarine to the underside of the broilers.

N.B. Fay used to cook her rice the night before and put it in the roaster, then add the broilers when she came home from her radio job around five. She used a woodstove and never timed them, but somehow they were just ready when ten or twelve guests trooped in. I have tried it with poultry stuffing as well as with instant rice, and can recommend it. The chicken juices drip down and give that extra special flavor. The dish is ready to serve when a fork slides into the breast without bringing any rosy juice back with it. From 30 to 45 minutes does it.

This is a Godsend for a buffet party because you can turn the oven low and the chicken and rice do not dry up. We favor it for guests who may arrive an hour late or may, on the other hand, turn up before we expect them!

Serve a grapefruit and avocado salad with this and cooked frozen peas with a can of sliced mushrooms added.

MY OWN BROILERS

½ broiler per person
1 bottle garlic French dressing, as needed
Butter or margarine

Marinate the broilers in the dressing for an hour or so. Drain. Place broilers on the broiler rack, but 4 inches from the unit. (This is unorthodox, I believe. Slower broiling makes for tenderness.)

Broil, turning once or twice and adding a little of the butter or margarine as needed. Baste once with the drained marinade. Broilers are done when the skin side turns golden brown and the underside is no longer pink. Take your time on this, many a broiler has been served with red juice still running out.

Serve on a hot platter garnished with toast triangles and sprigs of watercress, parsley, or bits of lettuce.

CHICKEN CACCIATORE

2 frying chickens (around 3 pounds each)
¼ cup flour
Salt and pepper
½ cup olive oil or salad oil (or half each)
1 large onion, chopped
1 carrot, chopped
1 clove minced garlic
1 can tomato purée (No. 2½)
½ cup dry white wine
2 tablespoons chopped parsley

Disjoint chickens, dredge with seasoned flour, and brown in the oil. Add onion, carrot, garlic and when onion is transparent, add tomato purée and wine. Cover and simmer about an hour, or until chicken is tender.

Add parsley and test for seasoning.

Serves 6.

N.B. This is perfect for an electric skillet which goes to the table for serving.

When using olive oil, be sure it is mild and fresh-tasting.

This recipe may be varied by using canned tomatoes, and adding chopped green pepper (¼ to ½ cup).

Either fluffy rice or broad noodles are in order.

CHICKEN DIVAN

1 large chicken, boiled, sliced
4 bunches broccoli, cooked
½ cup melted butter or margarine
½ cup flour
2 cups milk, heated
1 cup whipped cream
½ teaspoon Worcestershire
1½ tablespoons Parmesan cheese
1 jigger dry sherry
Salt and pepper to taste
½ cup Hollandaise sauce

Lay broccoli in a greased large flat casserole and cover with slices of the chicken. In a separate pan melt the butter or margarine, blend in the flour and add the milk, stirring until smooth and thickened. Add the cream, seasonings, wine and cheese, and the Hollandaise.

Pour the sauce over the chicken, sprinkle Parmesan cheese on top and run the casserole in the oven until hot. Turn the broiler on to brown the cheese. Add a dash of extra sherry before serving if you like.

Serves 10.

CHICKEN EN GELÉE

4 chicken breasts
1 can chicken consommé (or use bouillon cubes, dissolved)
2 stalks celery
3 scallions
2 small carrots, diced
4 cups water
Seasoning to taste
2 envelopes unflavored gelatin
1½ cups each cooked peas, lima beans, green beans, carrots

Simmer the chicken breasts in the water and consommé with the scallions, celery, carrot and seasonings. When tender (45-50 minutes) take out the chicken and chill. Strain and chill the broth separately, removing the fat when it rises. Then soften the gelatin in one cup of the broth, heat until dissolved, and add to remaining broth (you need 4 cups of broth in all).

Now take the bones from the chicken breasts, slice the breasts and arrange in a deep platter or serving dish. (A large glass rectangular dish will do.) Cover the chicken with the vegetables, and, when the gelatin is chilled until almost thick, spoon it gently over.

Chill thoroughly.

Serves 8.

STILLMEADOW FRIED CHICKEN

½ frying chicken to each person (you may use larger than
  usual for this method)
Eggs, beaten lightly (1 egg to each fryer)
Milk (1 tablespoon to an egg)
Flour and seasoned bread crumbs (these come in a package),
  half of each (¾ cup to each fryer)
Butter or margarine (2 tablespoons to each fryer)

Add the milk to the beaten eggs. Wipe the chicken with
a clean damp cloth. Dip in the egg and milk. Dip in the flour
and crumbs. Dip lightly again in the liquid to set the crumb
mixture. Let rest while you heat the heavy skillet or electric
frying pan with the butter or margarine. Dip again in the
crumb and flour mix and when the butter or margarine is bubbling hot (this is the best way I can describe it) lay the chicken
pieces in.

Brown until golden, lift with tongs or a spatula (do not
pierce with a fork and let those juices run out) turn and brown
the other side. Then turn the heat low and continue to cook
for 30-40 minutes. If the chicken shows signs of getting dry,
cover the pan. Add a little salad oil if needed.

Serve on a hot platter, and I do mean hot.

*N.B. This is a combination of Maryland fried chicken, Vir-
ginia fried chicken and New England fried chicken. It is not
according to any one rule. Also the covering is controversial.
But it happens to work for me.*

GRAVY:

For this, the chicken stays hot in the oven on a heat-proof
platter. I stir in flour, 1 tablespoon to 1 tablespoon of the
drippings and cracklings left in the pan. I then add the broth
from having cooked the neck, the giblets, a bit of celery top
and a slice of onion. If this turns out to be short of liquid, I
add thin cream or top milk. I do not let cream boil, this is

fatal. But when it simmers and is ready to boil, the gravy is done.

Fried chicken and cream gravy such as this needs tiny hot biscuits (I use a mix) because a split biscuit takes so well to extra gravy.

Serve a non-starchy vegetable such as spinach or asparagus or broiled tomatoes with this, a very crisp green salad with nothing but oil and vinegar on the side. And who wants dessert? Just reach for one more bite of chicken.

I sometimes, when hurried, do the seasoned-flour version. I shake the chicken up in a paper bag, praying it won't have a hole in it, with plenty of flour, salt, pepper, paprika, a dash of onion salt. Then I proceed as above.

I could never approximate my Virginia cook's fried chicken, but then, I never got the recipe. She said she just fried it, being careful. But the Stillmeadow fried chicken never seems to have any left-overs, so I shall have to settle for that.

CHICKEN WITH WINE

1 3-pound frying chicken, cut in quarters
2 tablespoons butter or margarine
½ cup dry white table wine
1 can (medium) mushrooms
1 cup cream
Salt, pepper, paprika
1 tablespoon orange juice

In a deep kettle, sauté the chicken in the butter until golden brown. Cover and cook slowly until tender (about 40 minutes), adding a little water if it gets dry. When the chicken is tender, keep it hot on a warm platter. Add the mushrooms to the juice in the kettle, and gradually add the wine. Stir cream in gradually, add seasonings and orange juice, and when hot and thick, pour over the chicken.

Serves 4.

RUSSIAN HUNTER'S CHICKEN

1 fricassee chicken, 4-5 pounds
1 clove garlic
1 sliced onion
1 minced green pepper
3 chopped carrots
3 stalks celery
1 No. 2 can tomatoes
Butter or margarine
Salt, pepper, paprika, oregano

Brown garlic, onion, pepper, carrots, celery (chopped) in a heavy skillet. Meanwhile brown the cut-up chicken in a Dutch oven or electric frying pan, using the butter or margarine. When the chicken is golden brown, pour the tomatoes over, add the remaining ingredients, seasonings. Cover tightly and cook until the chicken is about to fall from the bones. Then remove the bones, lift the chicken meat to a warm platter and pour the sauce over.

Serves 4-6.

N.B. Serve with broad noodles, boiled, fluffy rice or whipped potatoes. Green beans are good with it; but skip the salad. Needs no biscuits as everybody wants more noodles anyway. For dessert canned grapefruit sections laced with Crème de menthe.

I have made this in my pressure cooker often. I follow the fricassee-chicken directions, but I cut the timing by ¼th.

HAWAIIAN CHICKEN

1 cut-up frying chicken, 2-3 lbs.
1 egg, slightly beaten
1 cup fine bread or cracker crumbs
1 teaspoon salt
¼ teaspoon thyme
¼ teaspoon marjoram
½ teaspoon paprika

Mix crumbs with seasonings. Dip chicken in egg, then in the crumb mixture. Fry in ¼-inch-deep hot fat in skillet until brown. (Electric skillet is perfect for this.)
Drain off excess fat.

THE SAUCE:

1 cup pineapple juice
½ cup water
2 tablespoons lemon juice
1 tablespoon cornstarch
¼ teaspoon curry powder (I use more than this)
1 tablespoon sugar
1 cup pineapple bits
Slivered almonds

Combine the juices, cornstarch, curry and sugar. Cook until blended. Add the pineapple bits. Pour over the chicken, cover and cook slowly in oven or electric skillet (325° to 350°) for 30 minutes.

Arrange chicken on hot platter, pour the sauce over, and sprinkle with sliced blanched almonds.
Serves 4.

N.B. You can fry the chicken ahead of time, make the sauce, and combine for the baking while the guests sip their tomato juice or drinks.

ERMA VANEK'S CHICKEN PAPRIKASH

1 4-5-pound fowl, cut up.
Butter or margarine as needed.

In a Dutch oven or deep kettle, brown 1 large diced onion. When it is golden (but not brown) add 3 tablespoons paprika (the sweet Hungarian paprika if possible). Add the chicken, cover tightly, and when it begins to brown, add ½ cup water to make the steam, and cook until tender.

Add water if needed later.

When the chicken is tender, add I pint container sour cream. Do not let boil, or the cream separates.

THE DUMPLINGS:

Put 1 cup lukewarm water in a small mixing bowl. Break two eggs in and stir. Add the liquid to 2 cups flour sifted with 1 teaspoon salt.

Stir until it makes a soft dough—when it pulls away from the side of the bowl, it is ready.

Have a kettle of boiling water ready, and drop the dough into it in spoonfuls. Dip the spoon in the water between each dumpling to keep them from sticking together. Use a dessert or soup spoon so the dumplings will be small.

Cook dumplings about 7 minutes, then drain in a colander and add to the chicken. You may test the dumplings for doneness by breaking one in two.

Serves 4-6, depending on the size of the fowl.

HURRICANE DUCK

Left-over duck (or turkey or chicken)
1 box instant rice
1 can mushrooms (1 large or 2 small)
Diced green pepper and onion
Salt, pepper, paprika
Can condensed mushroom or chicken soup

Remove all meat from the bones of the duckling. Meanwhile bring the water to a boil for the rice (follow the directions on the package) over your charcoal grill in a 1-quart kettle. Set the grill in your fireplace hearth. When the rice is added, cover and set on the hearth for 10 minutes. Meanwhile sauté onion and pepper in another kettle over the grill, adding butter or margarine as needed. Add the cut-up duck. Add the rice and stir lightly. Then add as much of the condensed soup as necessary to make duck hurricane creamy. If it is too thick, add a little fresh or canned milk.

Cook until the duck is bubbling.

Serves according to how much duck you have and how many hungry people are waiting.

N.B. Adding a few ripe pitted olives, if you have them, is a fine idea. The hurricane duck will keep warm on the hearth while you boil enough water for instant coffee or tea. Serve with a tossed salad, if you have any greens, and fresh fruit for dessert, if you have any fresh fruit!

ROAST DUCKLING

Wipe with a damp clean cloth and place duckling on a rack in shallow open roasting pan, breast up.

Stuff wishbone cavity lightly, and fasten neck skin to back with skewer. Stuff body cavity, and close openings with skewers or cord. Tie drumsticks to body with a cord.

Roast in a slow oven (325°). Do not add water, and do not sear. Do not cover or baste. Spoon extra fat from the pan as it drips down.

Turn duckling, when almost done, to brown underparts. A 5-pound duckling takes 2½ to 3 hours' roasting; and always test for doneness by moving the drumstick. When it moves easily up and down, the meat is tender.

STUFFING:

You may use quartered tart apples, halved onions, celery for the stuffing. Or you may use your favorite bread stuffing. In this case skimp on the melted butter or margarine as the duckling has plenty of fat.

GRAVY:

You may make a regular gravy with the chopped cooked giblets stirred in. Or you may prefer:

ORANGE SAUCE:

2 tablespoons butter or margarine
2 tablespoons flour
1 cup water
¼ cup concentrated orange juice
Grated rind of one orange
Dash of salt
1 tablespoon sugar (or more if you want it very sweet)

Melt the fat over low heat, stir in flour and blend. Add the remaining ingredients and cook, stirring, until thickened.

Serve hot.

Serves 4.

ROCK CORNISH GAME HEN

6 small game hens, cleaned, fresh or frozen
3 tablespoons butter or margarine
3 tablespoons olive oil
2 cups dry white table wine
Salt and pepper to taste
6 shallots, chopped (or young green onion tops)
2 cups button mushrooms

Heat the oil and butter or margarine in a heavy pan. Brown the hens lightly, turning to brown evenly. Add wine and seasonings, cover, and cook for about 20 minutes (if frozen, cook until tender when pierced with a fork). Then add the shallots and mushrooms and cook 20 minutes longer.

Lay the birds on a hot platter and pour the sauce from the pan over them.

Serves 6.

TURKEY TETRAZZINI

2½ cups diced cooked turkey
½ pound spaghetti
4 tablespoons butter or margarine
4 tablespoons flour
2 cups well-seasoned turkey stock
½ pound fresh mushrooms, sliced
2 tablespoons butter or margarine
2 tablespoons sherry
1 cup table cream
½ cup Parmesan cheese, grated

Melt butter and blend in flour, cook until smooth. Add stock and cook until smooth and thick, stirring constantly. Sauté the mushrooms in 2 tablespoons butter or margarine, and add to sauce with the sherry and cream, and turkey.

Meanwhile cook the spaghetti in boiling salted water until tender. Drain. In a greased 8-by-12-inch baking pan, put half the spaghetti. Cover with half the turkey mixture. Add the rest of the spaghetti and turkey. Top with cheese. Bake in a moderate oven (350°) until browned and bubbly. (It takes about 25 minutes.)

Serves 6.

PAELLA

1 frying chicken, cut in serving pieces
1 package frozen jumbo shrimps (or 1 pound fresh shrimps,
    shelled and de-veined, or 2 medium sized cans
2 tablespoons flour
¼ cup salad or olive oil
1½ cups uncooked rice (the long grain, if possible)
1 medium onion, diced, or 2 small (about 1 cup)
1 clove garlic, crushed
1 medium green pepper, chopped
1 pimento, cut fine
1 box frozen peas, or 1 large can peas
4 tomatoes, peeled and cut in bite-size pieces
1 cup clam juice
½ cup chicken broth (use bouillon cube if you need to)
Salt, pepper, marjoram to taste
Butter or margarine
1 dozen fresh clams

Dredge the chicken in flour and sauté in the oil until lightly browned. Place in a deep 3-quart baking dish or casserole.

Sauté rice, with the next four ingredients, stirring frequently. When the rice is golden, spoon the mixture over the chicken. Add the peas and tomatoes.

Meanwhile place the scrubbed clams and 1 cup water in a large pan. Cover, heat to boiling, simmer 3 or 4 minutes, or until the shells open. Remove clams, strain the broth (you need a cupful). Heat clam juice with the seasonings and chicken broth, pour over mixture in the baking dish. Bake in a moderate oven (350°) 30 minutes, then add clams and shrimp, cover and bake 30 minutes longer, or until chicken and rice are fork tender.

N.B. If you need more liquid add extra chicken bouillon. Do not take the clams from their shells—they do something for this superb dish. But if you cannot get fresh clams, use 2 cans (7½ ounces each) and 1 bottle of clam juice.

Serves 6.

Vegetables

A GOOD MANY MEN, and some women too, say they do not care for vegetables. One of my best friends, when eating out, will push away the pale string beans and the rubbery dish of corn and say firmly, "This is my day to have scurvy." She will, however, eat three helpings of my Baked Zucchini and Tomatoes.

My own life with vegetable cooking began when we had a garden and suddenly the back kitchen overflowed with ripe tomatoes, squash, cabbages, sweet corn. From the first radish to the last Brussels sprout, we had vegetables. Vegetables for the family, vegetables to can, vegetables to give away. And still more vegetables.

At this point, I began to look for different ways to cook vegetables. And, the more I tried, the more interesting vegetable cooking became. For freshly picked vegetables sun-ripened in your garden, you can hardly go wrong, except that nobody wants string beans every night in the week, boiled.

Then I began to consider city people, for I had been one myself, who never have a fresh-picked vegetable with the sun still warming it. I knew what it was like to haunt the city groceries, hoping for some reasonably crisp vegetable. I knew how tired one can get of canned

144

vegetables heated up or frozen vegetables cooked according to directions.

The truth is that any vegetable, whether bought in a city mark-down market or canned or frozen or carried in from your own garden newly picked, can make good eating. It's what you do with it that counts.

For canned vegetables, which are an all-year-round help on the emergency shelves, even if you live in the country and raise your own, there are several tips.

First, drain the juice from the can, add seasonings (the canned vegetables have very little) and boil the juice down to about a half. Then add the vegetables and heat to simmering. Add a dab of butter or margarine, some freshly ground pepper and some seasoned salt. Add, for peas and beans, a little thin cream. Add a little rosemary to canned string beans. Add a can of chopped mushrooms to peas, beans or corn. Add a dash of sugar to lima beans, with butter or margarine. Add a mint leaf to canned peas. Sauté a bit of onion in butter or margarine and add to almost any canned vegetable.

For frozen vegetables, cook, covered, on low heat. You seldom need to add liquid, as the frost in the vegetables will provide moisture. If the vegetable needs more moisture, add a little water and a chicken bouillon cube. Cook frozen vegetables without thawing, with the exception of spinach, which I find is better thawed first.

But whether you carry your basket out as the dew dries, or open a can, or tear off the wax paper on a frozen vegetable, you can serve savory vegetables.

Out of more recipes than I can count, I have chosen a few very special Stillmeadow favorites for this exchange with neighbors.

BIBI'S BROCCOLI SOUFFLÉ

1½ cups chopped cooked broccoli, or asparagus, or spinach
3 eggs
1½ cups mild cheese, diced or grated
2 tablespoons butter or margarine
2 tablespoons flour
¾ cup milk
1 teaspoon chopped onion

Make cream sauce with butter or margarine, flour, milk. Add onion and cheese, stir until cheese melts. Add beaten egg yolks and vegetable. Fold in stiffly beaten whites of eggs. Turn into a greased casserole or baking dish, and bake in a moderate oven (350°) about an hour. Since this is like a custard, it helps to put the dish in a pan of hot water in the oven.

It is done when it begins to draw away from the side of the casserole or a knife inserted in the center comes out clean.

Serves 4-6.

N.B. *With a grilled ham steak, this makes company fare. Add fresh, chilled, sliced tomatoes bedded on lettuce and drizzled with garlic French dressing for the last word.*

BRAISED CELERY

1 bunch celery
Butter or margarine
½ cup chicken stock, or 1 chicken bouillon cube dissolved
    in ½ cup boiling water

Wash and separate the celery stalks. Cut in 3-inch pieces. Sauté gently in the butter or margarine until just beginning to brown. Add the stock, season with freshly ground pepper, cover, and cook until the celery is tender.

Serves 4-6.

N.B. Celery is a dieter's delight, but raw stalks do get tiresome.

KING'S ARMS CREAMED CELERY

1 bunch celery
Cream sauce
Chopped pecans

Separate, clean the celery, cut in bite-size pieces and cook in boiling, salted water until tender. Meanwhile make the cream sauce (see CREAM SAUCE). Place the celery in a greased casserole, pour the sauce over, and add chopped pecans (use ½ cup to a cup of cream sauce).

Top with buttered bread crumbs. Bake in a moderate oven (350°) until browned on top.

N.B. The amount is variable. 2 cups of cooked celery to 1 cup of cream sauce serves 4-6, but celery stalks do differ. I first had this in Williamsburg and begged the recipe from the Chef. He told me pecan halves would do equally well, and I tried it, and he was right! At King's Arms this was served with fried chicken, a tossed salad, hot cornsticks, and the Green Gage Plum Ice Cream.

BARBECUED CORN CASSEROLE

2 large cans whole-kernel corn, drained, or an equal amount
   frozen
8 frankfurters
1 8-ounce can Spanish tomato sauce
¼ cup lemon juice
4 tablespoons diced onion
1 teaspoon dry mustard
Salt and pepper to taste; dash garlic salt

Season the corn with salt and pepper and spread in the bottom of a greased casserole or baking dish. Prick the frankfurters with a fork and arrange on the corn. Mix the remaining ingredients and bring to boiling point. Pour over the frankfurters. Bake in a moderate oven (350°) for 25 to 30 minutes.

Serves 6.

CONNECTICUT CORN PUDDING

2 cups corn (canned, frozen or fresh)
6 strips bacon, fried until crisp and drained
½ green pepper, diced
1 small onion, diced
½ cup soft bread crumbs
2 eggs, beaten
2 cups top milk
1 teaspoon salt
½ cup buttered crumbs

Drain bacon on a paper towel. Then sauté the pepper and onion in 2 tablespoons of the bacon drippings. Add corn, bread crumbs, eggs, milk, seasoning and bacon broken in bits. Stir together and pour into a greased 1½-quart casserole. Top with buttered crumbs and bake in a moderate oven (375°) for about 40 minutes.

Serves 6.

N.B. This is a good supper dish, served with broiled tomatoes, a green salad, buttermilk biscuits (buy ready to bake) and coffee.

SAUTÉED EGGPLANT

1 medium eggplant
2 eggs, slightly beaten
Flour
Salt, pepper, paprika

Slice the eggplant without peeling in slices about ¼ inch thick. Dip the slices alternately in the egg, the flour, and season well.

Sauté in a heavy skillet with butter or margarine or bacon drippings. Turn once. When golden brown and tender to a fork, they are done.

Allow 2-3 slices per person according to how big the circumference of the slices.

N.B. There are many delicious ways to cook this purple fruit of the garden from stuffed, Creole, to Eggplant Caviar. But at Stillmeadow we serve it this way, since it is the only way I am not allergic (slightly) to it.

WILTED LETTUCE WITH SAUSAGE DRESSING

8 sausage links
1 head Boston lettuce
2 tablespoons vinegar
2 teaspoons sugar
½ teaspoon salt

Sauté sausages over low heat until brown. Drain on absorbent paper and cut in 1-inch lengths.

Pour off all but 6 tablespoons sausage fat. Add vinegar, salt and sugar, and heat to boiling. Pour over the lettuce, broken into bite-size pieces.

Add sausages last and toss gently. Serve immediately.
Serves 4.

BARBECUED LIMA BEANS

Soak 2 cups dried lima beans in cold water to cover overnight. Drain, cover with fresh cold water and cook until tender with ¼ pound diced salt pork, or an end of bacon.

Drain, reserving 1½ cups of the liquor.

1 sliced onion
1 clove garlic
¼ cup fat or drippings
1½ tablespoons dry mustard
2 tablespoons Worcestershire
1½ teaspoons chili powder
1 teaspoon salt
1 can tomato soup diluted with half a can of water
⅓ cup vinegar

Brown onion and garlic in fat. Add remaining ingredients and the liquor from the beans. Simmer five minutes. Place beans and sauce in a deep casserole, top with thin slices of salt pork, and bake in a hot oven (375°) for 30 minutes, adding more bean liquor if needed.

Serves 6.

N.B. This is a perfect main hot dish for a buffet. Thin sliced cold ham and salad do no harm. Lemon bisque adds the last touch.

GLAZED ONIONS

12 large onions, peeled
½ cup melted butter
⅔ cup honey
⅓ cup catsup

Parboil the onions in boiling, salted water until partly tender. Place them in a shallow baking dish (glass if you have it). Blend the remaining ingredients and pour over the onions.

Bake in a moderate oven (350°) until the onions are tender (test with a fork), and the glaze is thick and almost candied. Baste frequently.

Serves 8-10.

N.B. This is what we always serve with the Thanksgiving turkey and the Easter ham. I have known even non-onion eaters to take a second on this dish.

SUPPER ONIONS

1 large onion per person
Prepared stuffing
1 cup or more consommé or bouillon, as needed
Milk
Butter or margarine, melted

Peel the onions and with an apple-corer or a grapefruit knife remove the centers (save for soups or salads). Pack prepared stuffing well into the centers. Brush the onions with milk. Spoon a small amount of the butter or margarine in the centers of the onions, then place the onions in a greased shallow baking pan. Pour the consommé or bouillon around them. Bake in a slow oven (325°) until the onions are tender when pierced with a fork. Baste occasionally.

N.B. You may sprinkle grated Parmesan cheese on the tops just before the onions are done. Serve with broiled bacon or Canadian bacon, a green salad, and hot crusty poppy-seed rolls.

ONION PIE

8 onions sliced thin
3 tablespoons shortening
2 cups flour
2 teaspoons baking-powder
½ teaspoon salt
⅓ cup shortening
⅓ cup milk
1 egg
½ cup thin cream
Seasoning
6 or 7 broiled bacon strips

Cook onions in shortening until golden but not brown. Meanwhile sift the dry ingredients together, cut in the ⅓ cup shortening, work it in until the texture is like coarse cornmeal. Moisten with the milk. Mix into a ball, and knead on a floured board. Roll out and fit the dough into a 10-inch pie pan.

Spread the onions over when slightly cool, and season with salt and pepper.

Beat the egg with the cream and pour over all.

Bake 20 minutes at 450°, or a hot oven, or until the pie is slightly brown on top and the biscuit well done. Sprinkle bacon over the top and serve.

Serves 4-6.

N.B. This makes a one-dish luncheon with a green salad and coffee. If you want dessert, make it a light one.

POTATO PANCAKES

8 medium potatoes peeled and grated
Bouillon or beef stock
2 eggs
1 cup all-purpose flour, or more as needed
Salt, pepper, paprika to taste
Butter, margarine, or bacon drippings

Soak the grated potatoes in ice water for a few minutes, then drain and dry well on paper towels. Measure the pulp (the amount will vary according to the size of the potatoes).

Add an equal amount of bouillon or stock to the potatoes, then the eggs, slightly beaten, and the flour and seasonings. Beat well. (I hope you do have an electric beater.) Add more flour, beating constantly, until the batter has the consistency of regular pancake batter. Meanwhile heat the griddle with the fat on it, and when it is hot, drop the batter in spoonfuls on the griddle. Turn once to brown evenly.

Serves 6.

N.B. This is a lovely Sunday brunch dish. Crisp bacon or tiny sausages go well with it. A classic served with pot roast.

GREEN PEPPER BAKE

1 large green pepper per person

Cut off tops, remove seeds (watch them, they are fiery). Drop peppers in salted boiling water for 5 minutes.

Arrange in a casserole or baking pan.

For the stuffing, mix cooked rice with diced onion and canned cream celery soup. Pack in firmly, and top each pepper with a hat of deviled ham.

Bake in a moderate oven (375°) until bubbly.

N.B. You may add milk to the pan to keep the peppers moist or use tomato juice or a bit more of the celery soup, thinned with milk.

QUICK COUNTRY SCRAMBLE

1 package frozen potato patties
Butter or bacon drippings
6 eggs
Salt, pepper, dash Cayenne

Cook the potato patties in a heavy skillet in the butter or drippings, breaking them up as they cook, as for hashed-brown potatoes. Beat the eggs, add the seasonings. Turn the heat low under the potatoes, pour in the egg mixture and stir just until the eggs are set.

Serves 4.

N.B. Serve with catsup or chili sauce on the side. A good quick supper dish. Nice with broiled tomatoes and a tossed salad and coffee. Good garnished with crisp broiled bacon and a little fresh watercress.

RHODE ISLAND SUPPER POTATOES

5 medium potatoes, peeled and sliced thin
½ cup melted butter or margarine
1½ teaspoons Worcestershire
1¾ teaspoons salt
¼ teaspoon paprika

Cook potato slices in boiling salted water for 5 minutes. Drain, and spread them out in a greased baking pan. Pour over the butter or margarine mixed with the seasonings. Bake in a moderately hot oven (375°) until the potatoes are tender, basting frequently with the sauce.

Serves 4.

N.B. Serve with thinly sliced cold rare roast beef or sliced boiled ham or cold cuts. Orange and onion salad is a good accompaniment. (Slice oranges and onions thin, arrange on lettuce leaves, dress with plain French dressing.)

SCALLOPED POTATOES SUPREME

1 medium-sized potato per person, sliced thin
4 link sausages per person
½ onion per person, thinly sliced
Flour
Milk to cover
Grated Swiss, Parmesan or Cheddar cheese
Seasonings—salt, pepper, paprika

Use a flat baking dish, preferably glass. Grease it well. Arrange a layer of sliced potatoes in the bottom, next a layer of onion. Season this layer with salt, plenty of freshly ground pepper, paprika. Sprinkle flour over. Sprinkle some of the grated cheese over. Add another layer of potatoes, onions, seasonings and cheese, and a dusting of flour. When the final layer is in the dish, pour the milk over, to barely cover the top layer (heated milk will hurry up cooking time).

Bake in a moderate (350°) oven, covered. Meanwhile partly cook the sausages, just to get some of the fat out, but not all of it. When the potatoes have baked 25 minutes, arrange the drained sausages on top, remove the cover, and finish baking. When the potatoes are tender, it is done.

N.B. You may speed this up by boiling the potatoes and onions a few minutes in boiling salted water. This is an elegant dish, because the sausage flavors the whole. Serve with almost any vegetable such as peas, green beans or asparagus.

SWEET POTATO SOUFFLÉ

2 cups sweet potatoes, cooked and mashed
4 eggs, separated
½ cup milk
¼ cup rum or brandy
4 tablespoons butter or margarine
Salt, Cayenne
1½ teaspoons grated orange rind

Heat the milk, add the rum or brandy and the butter or margarine. Beat this mixture into the potatoes, adding the seasonings. Beat the egg yolks and add them. Fold in the egg whites, stiffly beaten.

Turn the mixture into a greased casserole. Bake in a hot oven (400°) for 25 minutes or until the soufflé is delicately browned. Serve at once.

Serves 4-6.

N.B. If you have an electric mixer, this is especially easy. If you haven't, beat the potatoes with a wooden spoon, then with a rotary beater after adding the liquid. Serve with sliced cold chicken or turkey, fresh or frozen asparagus dressed with butter (no Hollandaise this time). No sweet dessert either, but a bowl of fruit with the inevitable coffee.

STUFFED SUMMER SQUASH

Pattypan squash (sometimes called Cimling)
Salt, pepper, paprika
Stuffing

Use the young small Pattypan squash. Scrub them, and put whole in boiling, salted water. Cook until the shell is slightly soft. Remove from water, and cool slightly. Then remove a round section from the stem end and scrape out the seeds. Season the inside of the squash shell with salt, pepper, paprika. Fill with the stuffing and bake in a hot oven about 20 minutes or until the squash is tender to a fork and the stuffing bubbles.

STUFFING:

Use prepared poultry stuffing moistened with top milk, or creamed tuna or creamed chicken or creamed peas with mushrooms. Dot with butter or margarine, and sprinkle grated Parmesan cheese on top.

N.B. If you must use squash larger than a butter plate, pour a little milk in the baking dish to help tenderize the shell.

This makes a perfect luncheon dish with fresh fruit salad and hot corn muffins and coffee.

SAVORY SUMMER SQUASH

Summer squash
¼ cup grated cheese, Cheddar or American
3 tablespoons grated onion
Salt, pepper, paprika

Slice the squash thin. You should not have to peel it unless it is tough. In that case, remove the center seed portions, too.

Arrange the slices in a greased baking pan, slightly overlapping them. Dot generously with butter or margarine, then sprinkle onion and cheese over.

Add seasonings. Broil 4 inches from the broiler unit until nicely browned and the squash is tender.

A medium squash serves 4.

SPINACH DE LUXE

1 box frozen chopped spinach
½ can condensed cream of mushroom soup

Cook the spinach as directed on the package, and, when it is nearly done, stir in the soup. Heat until it bubbles, stirring constantly.

Serves 2-3.

N.B. I take a stand on cooking frozen spinach. It should be partially thawed. Otherwise part of it is overcooked before the center has dreamed of thawing. It's easy enough to move that frozen spinach to the lower part of your refrigerator in the morning or the night before. But put a pan under it, as I have yet to find the frozen food of any category that won't leak through the package in time.

This is a very easy but glorified version of creamed spinach and the slight aura of mushroom does no harm at all.

SPINACH TIMBALES

3½ cups cooked spinach (fresh, frozen, or canned)
3 eggs, slightly beaten
Salt and pepper to taste
4 slices bacon, diced

Fry bacon until crisp and add the drained spinach. Then add eggs and seasonings. Turn into greased custard cups or ramekins and bake in a moderate oven (350°) until set. This takes around 35 minutes, according to the size of your containers. Unmould and serve with cheese, or with a cream sauce, or with cream of mushroom soup, heated and diluted with half a can of milk.

Serves 6.

FRIED TOMATOES

Ripe or green tomatoes
Wash and cut in half
Flour or cornmeal, enough to dredge tomato slices
Salt and pepper
Bacon fat, or butter, or margarine, or cooking oil

Add seasonings to flour or cornmeal and dredge the tomato halves in it. Heat the fat until it is hot but not burning. (A heavy skillet is best.)

Fry the tomatoes, turning once. When they are tender to a fork and browning, remove them from the fire and lay them on a hot platter. Keep warm while you make the gravy.

Stir 2 tablespoons flour into the drippings (or more, according to number you are serving). Add 1 cup top milk or evaporated milk and stir until the gravy boils up and is smooth. Pour over the tomatoes.

Allow two tomatoes per person. The gravy amounts above make gravy for 2-3 people. Increase amount according to how many you are serving.

If you use green tomatoes, unripe, add a dusting of sugar after you flour them.

Serve on toast triangles.

N.B. For a supper one-dish meal, fry bacon until crisp, remove bacon, and fry the tomatoes. Make the gravy, lay the tomatoes on a hot platter, pour gravy over, top with the crisp bacon.

FRIED TOMATO BAKE

Fried tomatoes, 1 medium to a person or 2 small
Butter or margarine
Buttered crumbs
Parsley, chopped
Salt, pepper

Fry the tomatoes (see recipe). Arrange them in layers in a deep greased casserole or baking dish. Top with buttered crumbs, dot with butter or margarine. Bake in a hot oven (400°) for 20 minutes or until bubbly. Add parsley 5 minutes before you take from the oven.

N.B. This is a life-saver for the last-minute cook. Who wants to stand watching frying tomatoes (and you cannot leave them a minute) when guests are in the living-room having fun? Well, not I. Who wants to take time to fry tomatoes when getting in late from work? These may be fried the night before and put in the casserole ready to bake. Just take them from the refrigerator in time to warm the casserole, if it is glass or earthenware, before subjecting it to the hot oven. You will find that the tomatoes, served carefully, give the illusion of being just fried, and the dish is far, far better than any stewed tomato I ever met.

MISS EDDY'S WALNUT CROQUETTES

2 eggs, slightly beaten
3 tablespoons cream
1 cup soft bread crumbs
1 cup hot riced or mashed potatoes
1 cup finely ground walnuts
1 teaspoon each salt, grated onion, grated celery

Mix eggs, cream, and crumbs.

In another bowl mix potatoes (no butter or cream when you mash them) walnuts, seasonings. Work into first mixture making a stiff mass. Divide into 8 equal parts and shape into balls.

Then roll in more soft bread crumbs (1½ cups is enough) then in beaten egg, then in crumbs. Fry in deep fat at 375° until the croquettes are golden brown. Makes 8.

N.B. Miss Eddy was a gentle lavender-and-lace old lady, a French scholar and teacher. She used to have me for lunch and treat me as a grown-up although I was in the pigtail age. Her walnut croquettes were my favorite luncheon dish. She had salad with them and fine China tea.

BAKED ZUCCHINI

Zucchini
Ripe tomatoes
Onion, diced
Butter or margarine
Parmesan cheese, grated
Buttered crumbs
Salt, pepper, paprika

Allow 1 small zucchini (about the size of a large ripe cucumber) to 2 persons. Allow at least 1 tomato to 2 persons.
Slice the zucchini thin (do not peel). Remove stems from tomatoes and slice them. Arrange a layer of the zucchini slices in a greased casserole or baking pan. Season well. Sprinkle diced onion over. Lay slices of tomatoes on top of the zucchini, and season again. Add more diced onion. Repeat the process so you have 4 layers. Sprinkle the top layer generously with the cheese. Cover and bake 20-25 minutes in a medium hot oven (375°).

N.B. If you use a rectangular baking pan, make a cover of aluminum foil.
This is fine with grilled chops, a relish tray of crisp carrot sticks, cucumber sticks, celery or whatever you have that gives a crisp texture to complement the casserole.

RICE

I have probably served more gummy, gluey rice in my life than would be needed to cement a house foundation. I have spent a good many hours scrubbing rice from ruined pans too. By the time I got the rice off, so was the bottom of my kettle.

Fluffy, dry rice is as important as a smooth cream sauce or a gravy without lumps. It is a foundation dish for everything from casseroles to puddings. And when I began to cook, I assumed that anybody could cook rice. But when I began to entertain, some of my most nervous moments were concerned with whether the rice would be ALL RIGHT this time. Sometimes the kernels would be separate, tender, and dry. Sometimes they stuck together and to the pan better than postage stamps ever stick to an envelope.

For a time, I lowered my battle flag in the bottom of the last kettle I threw in the garbage, and settled for noodles, macaroni and spaghetti. But then I came back to try again. I have now cooked rice in a pressure cooker, a fancy electric double-boiler unit, a big kettle, a covered heavy skillet.

I also have used Minute Rice, which is a help for a hurry-up meal, and belongs on every kitchen shelf, beside the long-grain California and the brown rice.

Herewith my favorite ways to cook rice.

BOILED RICE

1 cup uncooked long-grain rice
2¼ cups fresh water
1 teaspoon salt, or seasoned salt
1 teaspoon lemon juice, fresh, frozen, canned

Bring the water to a rolling boil in a large kettle. Add seasoning and lemon juice. Now gently shake in the rice. When it is all in, stir once with a fork, and, when it begins to simmer again, turn the heat LOW, and cover the kettle tightly.

Cook over low heat for 25 minutes.

N.B. If you want very dry rice, remove the cover during the last 5 minutes of cooking. (I always do this anyway, just in case all the water is absorbed and you know what.) Turn off the heat, shake the kettle over the burner a couple of minutes, add butter or margarine, and if you cannot serve at once, keep warm in the oven.

We like to dust the top with curry powder.

BAKED CURRIED RICE

1½ cups raw rice
2 tablespoons of butter or margarine
2 teaspoons salt
¾ teaspoons curry powder
3 cups boiling water

Place the first four ingredients in a baking dish big enough for 8 cups. Better grease it first. Pour boiling water over, mix lightly with a fork, and cover.

Bake in hot oven (425°) about 25 minutes.

Uncover, fluff rice with fork, top with a bit more butter or margarine (or Parmesan cheese if you are worrying about the calories).

Serves 6.

N.B. This is an easy way to save current or fuel if you have a roasting chicken in the oven anyway.

173

SPANISH RICE

1 cup raw rice
6 slices bacon, cut fine
1 medium onion, diced
2½ cups canned tomatoes
Salt, pepper, paprika
1 clove garlic, crushed
2 green peppers, minced

In a heavy kettle sauté the bacon until crisp. Remove bacon. Add rice and cook, stirring, until it begins to brown. Then add the onion and continue to cook, stirring until the onion is golden. Add the bacon, and the rest of the ingredients.

Cover and cook slowly until the rice is tender (40 minutes to 1 hour). Keep the heat low. If necessary add more tomato toward the end of the cooking time.

PILAF

1 box long-grain or brown or regular white rice
1 medium onion, diced
1 clove garlic, minced
Butter or margarine or olive or salad oil
Chicken broth or consommé as needed
½ teaspoon saffron, soaked in ½ cup warm water 30 minutes

Melt the fat in a heavy skillet (iron or cast aluminum, preferably). When it is hot, add onion and garlic and cook until the onion is golden. Now add the rice and cook, stirring with a wooden spoon until the grains are beginning to brown. Add more fat if the rice begins to burn. Meanwhile bring the broth to a boil, and then pour over the rice. You will need to cover the rice about 1½ inches. Add saffron. Cover the skillet, reduce the heat to very low, and cook until the broth has all been absorbed and the rice is tender. Now taste for seasoning and add salt if necessary (the broth may be salty enough).

Serves 6.

N.B. This has a rich nutty flavor and is delicious with chicken or lamb or shrimp.

Sauces

A GOOD SAUCE often saves the dish. And I suppose there are enough different sauces being made around the world to float the Queen Mary. When I went to Paris, I gained five pounds in spite of hiking miles in the Louvre, because the French sauces were so delicious. Later on, I watched Dione Lucas, of Cordon Bleu fame, make sauces for fish, sauces for chicken, and sauces for desserts. Even her thick sauces were clear as crystal, and oh, the smell of herbs and wine and spices!

But if I made a good French sauce, I never had time to get anything ready to eat with it. So that was that. At this same time, a friend of mine decided to make Miss Lucas's brioche which involves, among a lot of other things, eight rollings of the dough. Eventually the dough is the size of a card table but as thin as a maple leaf. My friend spent all day making the brioches and got them in the oven around 5 P.M. By then she was so tired, she dropped down to rest a minute. The smell of the burning brioches woke her. She did save the pan.

She went back to biscuits and I went back to easy sauces. A smooth and delicate cream sauce is basic, I think. Once you can make that, you have no trouble with other sauces.

A word about vinegar. Some modern vinegars are almost pure acetic acid. If you are using this type of vinegar dilute with water a third to a half. Wine and herb vinegars do not need diluting.

CREAM SAUCE

    2 tablespoons butter or margarine
    2 tablespoons flour
    1 cup warm milk
    Salt, pepper, paprika to taste

Melt the butter or margarine over medium heat. Blend in the flour and stir until smooth, then add the milk gradually, and the seasonings, stirring constantly. When it is thick and smooth, it is done.

N.B. Use a French whisk if possible. Most hardware stores carry them now and the size for sauce-making costs 29 cents. There are only two tricks, keep the heat low, and stir. The flour should be cooked enough so the sauce will not taste of raw flour, and the slow cooking of butter and flour does it. Having the milk warm makes it blend easier.

BÉCHAMEL SAUCE

2 cups milk
4 tablespoons butter or margarine
½ small onion, finely minced
4 tablespoons flour

Bring the milk to a boil in a double boiler. Meanwhile simmer the onion in the butter or margarine until golden but not brown. Stir in the flour, then gradually add the hot milk, and keep stirring until smooth. Simmer 15 minutes until the flour is well cooked, stirring now and then. Strain through a fine sieve and serve as desired.

N.B. You may use equal parts milk and stock (fish or vegetable) depending on how you are going to use the sauce.

GOURMET BÉCHAMEL SAUCE

Make the sauce as above, then add 1 beaten egg yolk and reheat but do not boil. (If eggs are pullet-size, add two yolks.)

BREAD SAUCE

1 medium onion studded with cloves
2 cups milk
Dash of Cayenne
Salt
1 cup fresh bread crumbs
Butter or cream if desired

Put the onion, milk and seasonings in a pan or double boiler. Bring to a boil, and boil 5 minutes. Remove the onion and clove.

Add the crumbs—use more if you need to thicken the milk. Correct the seasoning. Add a little butter or cream if you wish a rich sauce.

N.B. This is delicious with roast game, chicken or Rock Cornish game hens.

BEURRE NOIR (BLACK BUTTER)

½ cup vinegar
1 bay leaf
1 cube butter
1 tablespoon parsley, minced

Boil the vinegar and bay leaf until it is reduced to half. Cook the butter until deep brown. Remove bay leaf from the vinegar and combine vinegar and butter. Add the parsley.

N.B. Serve with eggs, sweetbreads, brains.

CUCUMBER SAUCE

1 cucumber
½ teaspoon salt
2 tablespoons vinegar
1 cup thick cultured sour cream
1 tablespoon minced green onion or chives
Pepper

Peel and remove seeds from the cucumber, then grate it. Add the salt and let stand in the refrigerator for an hour or more. Drain well. Combine with the vinegar, sour cream, onion, pepper. Taste for salt.

N.B. Serve with baked-fish dishes.

HORSERADISH SAUCE

2 cups tart applesauce
½ cup prepared bottled horseradish

Combine. Serve cold.

N.B. Serve with roast goose, duck, pork, or cold meats. If you are lucky enough to have fresh horseradish add 2 tablespoons vinegar.

MINT SAUCE

½ cup fresh mint, finely chopped
½ cup vinegar
1 tablespoon sugar

Combine vinegar and mint and sugar and heat over a medium heat for 5 minutes. Serve hot.

N.B. Serve with lamb or mutton.

HOLLANDAISE SAUCE

½ cup butter or margarine
4 egg yolks
¼ cup light cream
¼ cup lemon juice, fresh, frozen or canned
½ teaspoon salt
Pinch of Cayenne

Heat the butter in the top of a double boiler, and set over boiling water when melted. Add the salt, Cayenne, and lemon juice to the egg yolks, and stir. (Don't beat the yolks.) Stir the yolk mixture into the hot butter, turn the heat down until the water in the bottom of the boiler is barely boiling.

Beat egg mixture with a rotary beater until thickened. Add the cream and continue to beat 2 minutes longer. Remove from heat.

N.B. This is so much easier than the traditional method of cutting ½ cup butter into 3 pieces and so on. Works, too.

SAUCE MORNAY

Make cream sauce according to the directions.
When it is done, lower the heat and gradually add:

2 tablespoons butter or margarine
2 tablespoons grated Parmesan cheese
2 tablespoons grated Swiss or mild Cheddar
Dash of Cayenne

WESTERN VIEW MUSTARD SAUCE

2 egg yolks
½ cup sugar
2 tablespoons dry mustard
1 teaspoon salt
1 large can evaporated milk, or 1 pint thin cream
½ cup vinegar

Beat the egg yolks and stir in the sugar, mustard and salt.
Add a little of the milk or cream to make a smooth mixture.
Meanwhile heat the rest of the milk or cream in the top of a
double boiler, but do not let it boil. When it is hot, add the
egg mixture and stir constantly until it thickens. When it
thickens, take from the fire, and stir in the vinegar slowly,
then return to the stove and continue cooking until the sauce
is creamy and thick. This takes about 5 minutes, and you must
watch it at this point and stir.

Since it is extra good, you won't mind hanging over it briefly
to be sure it doesn't boil up and separate.

Serve hot.

*N.B. This is the best sauce for ham. Next day you can serve
it cold on the left-over ham, and it is delicious on any cold
sliced meat or in sandwiches. It is also good added to salad
dressing.*

MUSTARD SAUCE

½ cup melted butter or margarine
½ cup prepared mustard
½ cup dry white table wine
½ cup fish stock
2 egg yolks
¼ cup vinegar
1 tablespoon sugar

Cook in a double boiler over barely boiling water until thick and smooth. Stir frequently. Serve hot.

N.B. Serve with bass or any white fish.

ORANGE GINGER SAUCE

1 cup orange juice
¼ cup sherry
¼ cup vinegar
¼ cup sugar
2 tablespoons soy sauce
1 tablespoon grated orange peel
1 tablespoon fresh ginger, shredded
2 tablespoons melted butter or margarine
2 tablespoons cornstarch

Mix all ingredients and cook until thick and clear, stirring constantly.

N.B. Serve with pork or chicken.

SMILEY BURNETTE'S REMOULADE SAUCE

1 cup mayonnaise
1 cup catsup
1 teaspoon Worcestershire
1 teaspoon prepared mustard
½ teaspoon salt
Dash Tabasco
½ small onion, diced

Blend in an electric blender or beat with a rotary beater until smooth.

N.B. This is perfect for shrimp, crab, lobster. Or add sour cream for a special salad dressing. Or add cream cheese and stuff celery with it.

CORDON BLEU SOUR-CREAM DRESSING

2 teaspoons salt
3 teaspoons fresh pepper
1 teaspoon crushed garlic or ½ teaspoon garlic salt
1 teaspoon lemon juice
8 tablespoons tarragon vinegar
4 tablespoons cider vinegar
3½ cups sour cream
1 teaspoon dry mustard
½ teaspoon Worcestershire sauce

Beat all together and use for salads.

N.B. Dione Lucas, that matchless cook, used this in a cooking class and I never forgot it. Of all the versions of sour-cream dressings, this is the most distinctive I have found.

SPECIAL FRENCH DRESSING

½ cup red wine vinegar (or tarragon or cider, if you wish)
1 cup olive oil (you may use part salad oil)
1 crushed clove garlic
4 teaspoons dry mustard
4 teaspoons salt
½ teaspoon paprika
Freshly ground pepper to taste
Pinch of Cayenne

Steep a pinch of salad herbs in the vinegar. Cool, mix vinegar and dry ingredients. Add the oil and shake.

For fruit salads, add a little sugar to the dry ingredients.

PARTY BARBECUE SAUCE

2 tablespoons chili powder
2 tablespoons paprika
¼ tablespoon Cayenne
1 tablespoon prepared mustard
1 tablespoon Worcestershire
1 pint cider vinegar
1 pint water
1 small onion diced
1 pint catsup

Place in a deep kettle and boil gently for 30 minutes. Stir constantly.

This is sauce enough for portions for 10 people.

N.B. Use on hamburger, broiled chops, broiled chicken, in barbecued sandwiches. Excellent added to baked beans for a picnic supper.

Salads

THE TRUE TEST of a meal is the salad. Limp, watery greens with a shredded carrot and a pale slice of tomato, such as you get too often at restaurants and hotels, are not salad. The idea that men won't eat salad may have come from such a dish.

Salad greens should be chilled and crisp. In the country, we gather them fresh: chicory; endive; Oak Leaf, Bibb, and May King lettuce; young spinach. We wash them under cold running water, drain them, wrap in a clean towel and put in the refrigerator. When we prepare them for salad, we tear the leaves by hand, never cut them.

If you have to buy store greens, soak them in cold water to which you have added ice cubes. For head lettuce pull the leaves apart from the core. Soak an hour or so.

I keep a wooden salad bowl for the green salads. I rub it with a cut clove of garlic now and then, and add a little pure olive oil, which I wipe around the bowl with a paper towel. I clean the bowl with a damp cloth after using.

For dressing, I like to make it in the bowl, then add the greens and toss with the wooden salad servers. There are now some excellent commercial dressings of various kinds. When I use them, I usually add something of my own, a bit of sour cream to the French dressings, garlic powder to a bland dressing, a dash of dry mustard, or a dollop of chili sauce. Crumbled cheese, chopped onion, minced celery leaves, and sieved hard-cooked egg yolks help many a salad.

For fruit salads I use an earthenware or glass bowl. Don't ask me why, it tastes better that way.

PARTY CHICKEN SALAD

1 large chicken, cooked
1 large cucumber, peeled and chopped
1 cup walnut meats, chopped
1 can French peas, drained
3 cups celery, diced
Mayonnaise

Remove the meat from the chicken and cut in pieces, but do not dice it. Add the rest of the ingredients and mix lightly with mayonnaise. Use just enough mayonnaise to give a good consistency but not sloppy. Turn into a bowl and chill thoroughly. When ready to serve, place the salad on a chilled platter with crisp lettuce around it. Garnish with strips of pimento, or chopped ripe olives, or green pepper rings, or tomato slices, or watercress.

Serves 6-8 or more, according to the size of the chicken.

You may use frozen chicken breasts for extra elegance. If so, steam them until tender, adding a little dry white wine while cooking.

SALAD BUFFET

1 pound shrimp
Salt, parsley, celery leaves, peppercorns
2 heads fresh lettuce, pulled in pieces
2 tablespoons diced onion
2 tablespoons diced green pepper
2 cups diced celery
1 diced alligator pear
2 shredded carrots

Cook the shrimp in boiling salted water with parsley, celery, peppercorns. Cook 25 minutes, drain, shell, de-vein. (You may substitute frozen canned shrimp.) Toss the lettuce with the next five ingredients and then add the shrimp. (Chill it if fresh.)

DRESSING:

1 cup mayonnaise
4 tablespoons catsup
2 tablespoons chili sauce
1 tablespoon prepared mustard
6 drops Tabasco
½ teaspoon pepper
½ tablespoon salt
2 tablespoons vinegar

Mix well, and pour over the salad.

Rub a large bowl with a clove of garlic, arrange whole lettuce leaves in it, then add the salad. Garnish with tomato wedges dipped in sharp French dressing and 1 alligator pear, peeled and sliced, dipped in French dressing or lemon juice.
Serves 4-6.

N.B. With hot French bread, a meal for the men.

188

LOUELLA'S JELLIED CUCUMBER SALAD WITH SHRIMPS

3 packages cooked frozen shrimp (or four 5½-oz. cans or equal amount fresh)
3 large or 4 medium cucumbers, peeled, seeded and grated (You need 4 cups of pulp and juice)
2 envelopes unflavored gelatin
½ cup cold water
1½ cups boiling water
1 tablespoon salt
½ teaspoon hot Mexican pepper sauce
¼ teaspoon pepper
Juice of 2 lemons
2 medium onions grated
Mayonnaise
Chili sauce

Soften gelatin in cold water, add the boiling water and stir until thoroughly dissolved. Add seasonings and lemon juice. Let cool, then add the cucumber and onions. Taste for seasoning. Add a few drops of green coloring if necessary. Pour into a 6-cup ring mould and chill until set. Turn out on a round platter. Mix shrimp with mayonnaise and add chili sauce enough to make it pink. Pile shrimp in the center of the cucumber jelly.
Serves 10.

N.B. Especially fine for a hot August night when company comes.

RUTH SANFORD'S CURRY RING

    3 cups cooked rice
    2 tablespoons butter or margarine
    3 tablespoons curry
    Mayonnaise enough to hold together the rice

Melt butter or margarine, stir in curry and simmer a minute or more. Blend into rice. Add mayonnaise and pack in a ring mould. Set in refrigerator overnight.

Turn out on a platter, and fill the center with chilled cooked jumbo shrimp or cut-up cooked lobster. Serve with a dressing combining sour cream and mayonnaise in equal parts.

Chutney as a side dish is a must.

Serves 4-6.

N.B. This is tops for a party luncheon. Serve tiny hot biscuits and coffee. Fruit compote for dessert.

EGGS IN ASPIC

8 eggs
½ cup liver paté or deviled ham
2 envelopes unflavored gelatin
½ cup cold water
4 cups chicken broth (canned, or made with bouillon cubes
   if you have no fresh stock)
1 tablespoon dried tarragon
Mayonnaise
Dry mustard

Soak gelatin in cold water 5 minutes. Meanwhile heat the broth. Dissolve the gelatin in the broth. Cool. Then cover the bottom of a mould (or use 8 ramekins or custard cups) with a layer of the gelatin. Sprinkle the tarragon over.

Poach the eggs, trim the edges, and let them cool. When the gelatin is slightly firm, slip the eggs in carefully. Spread them lightly with the paté. Then spoon the remaining gelatin over and set in the refrigerator until firm. Turn out on a bed of shredded salad greens. Season mayonnaise with mustard to taste, and serve in a bowl with the aspic. Garnish with watercress.

Serves 8.

N.B. *When my daughter tried this, she said the eggs kept floating and would not be pinned down. The secret is to let the gelatin set partially.*

FROZEN FRUIT SALAD

3 cups diced fruit (pineapple, peach, pear, melon balls or whatever)
½ cup white grapes
1 banana, diced
1 tablespoon unflavored gelatin
¼ cup water
3 tablespoons lemon juice
1 cup mayonnaise
1 cup cream, whipped (or see note under CHOCOLATE CREAM)

Soften the gelatin in the cold water, then dissolve over hot water. Combine the fruits and add lemon juice and gelatin. Put in the refrigerator until it begins to thicken. Then fold in mayonnaise and whipped cream. Turn into the biggest refrigerator tray and freeze in the freezing unit.

To serve, cut in squares and serve in lettuce cups with extra dressing.

Serves 6-8.

N.B. Canned fruit cocktail or frozen fruits may be used. But always have some fresh fruit with the canned.

LOBSTER MOUSSE

1 large can lobster
⅔ cups mayonnaise
1 tablespoon unflavored gelatin
1 tablespoon cold water
2 tablespoons boiling water
1 cup heavy cream, whipped
Salt

Soften the gelatin in the cold water, add the boiling water and stir. Cool. Add to the whipped cream, then salt to taste. Stir well.

Spread a layer of cream over the bottom and sides of a greased mould. Set in the refrigerator until it begins to thicken slightly. Meanwhile mix the lobster and mayonnaise, and season to taste. Gently place the lobster mixture in the mould, and put the remaining cream over the top. Chill until firm.

Serves 6-8.

N.B. *This may be made the day before, covered with aluminum foil and stored in the refrigerator.*

LIME RING

1 package lime gelatin
1 cup cottage cheese
3 tablespoons lemon juice or mild vinegar

Substitute the lemon juice or vinegar for 3 tablespoons of the water in which you dissolve the gelatin. Add the cottage cheese to the gelatin when it is just beginning to set. Mix lightly. Turn into a ring mould (rinse the mould with cold water). Chill until firm.

Serves 6.

N.B. This is so easy and so good. For a buffet try this at one end of the table, and the Tomato Cheese Mould at the other.

SMILEY'S PICNIC SALAD

1 large can fruit salad
1 banana
½ cup white seedless grapes
2 packages raspberry gelatin

Drain the fruit salad. Heat the juice to boiling and use it for part of the water in dissolving the gelatin. Follow the directions on the package for dissolving. Pour into a mould and set in the refrigerator until it begins to thicken. Add the fruit, and chill again until set.

Serves 6.

N.B. Smiley makes this in a hurry for an impromptu picnic by setting the mould in the freezing unit of the refrigerator until it begins to set.

This is a simple but refreshing salad to serve with charcoal-grilled pork chops and crusty garlic bread.

HOT POTATO SALAD

6 cups cooked potatoes, sliced thin
1 cup finely chopped onion
2 tablespoons minced parsley
⅔ cup vinegar
⅓ cup hot water
1 teaspoon sugar
1 beaten egg
⅓ cup salad oil
2 teaspoons salt (level)
Pepper to taste
1½ teaspoons monosodium glutinate

Combine onion, potatoes, parsley. Combine water and vinegar and heat to boiling, then add sugar.

Add hot mixture slowly to egg, then oil and seasonings. Beat with a rotary beater and, when well blended, pour over the potato and onion mixture. Stir gently and let stand in a warm place 15 minutes.

Serves 6-8.

N.B. If the potatoes are cold, set the salad in a warm oven or over a pan of hot water until the potatoes are heated through.

MARTHA FITZGERALD'S POTATO SALAD

3 pounds potatoes, peeled and diced
8 tablespoons olive oil
2 tablespoons vinegar
2 teaspoons salt
½ teaspoon freshly ground pepper
½ teaspoon red pepper
1 teaspoon prepared mustard
2 tablespoons chopped parsley
2 tablespoons chopped onion
4 tablespoons sherry

Cook the diced potatoes in boiling salted water until tender.
Put in a warm bowl.

Mix the other items well and pour over the potatoes.

Serve hot, lukewarm, or cold.

Serves 6-8.

N.B. This is the cook's best friend in the matter of potato salads. It does not have to be made at the last minute. Standing only enhances the flavor. Perfect for picnics because you won't worry about keeping it icy cold.

TOMATO CHEESE MOULD

1 tablespoon unflavored gelatin (1 package)
½ cup cold water
1 can tomato soup, boiling
1 cup cottage cheese
½ cup heavy cream, whipped
½ cup mayonnaise

Soften the gelatin in the cold water, then add to the hot soup. Let cool. Beat in the cottage cheese. Fold in the cream and mayonnaise and pour in a ring mould which you have rinsed in cold water. Chill. Unmould on a round chop platter. Serve extra mayonnaise in a small bowl in the center, and garnish with crisp lettuce.

Serves 6.

N.B. This always calls for seconds.

TUNA SALAD MOULD

2 cans tuna (6-ounce size)
2 hard-cooked eggs, diced
½ cup chopped ripe olives
1 tablespoon grated onion, or 1½ tablespoons minced chives
1 tablespoon unflavored gelatin
¼ cup cold water
2 cups mayonnaise

Soften the gelatin in the cold water 5 minutes, then dissolve over hot water and stir into the mayonnaise until well blended. Mix the tuna, eggs and olives, flaking the tuna with a fork into small pieces. Add onion or chives. Then mix the fish with the mayonnaise, turn into a mould and chill until firm.

Serves 6.

N.B. This is equally good with salmon or left-over cooked fish such as flounder. Taste for seasoning; fresh fish will need more.

TWENTY-FOUR-HOUR SALAD

2 eggs, beaten
4 tablespoons vinegar
4 tablespoons sugar
2 tablespoons butter
2 cups white cherries, cut in half
2 oranges (Remove rind and membranes. Cut oranges in
   pieces.)
2 cups pineapple chunks, canned or fresh
2 cups marshmallows, cut in pieces with scissors
1 cup cream

Put the eggs in the top of a double boiler over boiling water. Add vinegar and sugar, beating constantly until thick and smooth. Remove from heat, add butter, and let cool.

When cool, fold in cream, whipped until stiff, and the fruits. Chill in refrigerator overnight.

Serves 12.

N.B. This recipe was sent to me by my friend Elizabeth Baker and she admits it is very rich, but delicious, which it certainly is. You may always go on a diet the day after the party.

Pancakes, Breads, Pastry

THERE CAN BE NOTHING better than a fresh homemade loaf of bread, with the edges a little irregular and very crisp. This comes hot from the old iron range, and is sliced at once. Sweet country butter is at hand, and a comb of white-clover honey. We used to make our bread and I could hardly wait for it to be done. Jill made a rye loaf with honey that melted if you just looked at it, it was so tender. It had also whole wheat flour in it, which was ground at a nearby mill.

Nowadays, we settle for quick breads, for days seem to be growing shorter. Or we are busier than we were.

With modern mixes, and partly cooked light rolls, we can cook in a hurry and still have good eating. Pastry, pancake, muffin and waffle mixtures are always available and a wonderful addition to a busy cook's life.

The Italian and French breads are now in most stores, and poppyseed and sesame rolls. And so we fare well, even though I cast a nostalgic glance back to that loaf coming from the oven.

CHEESE BREAD

¼ cup shortening
⅓ cup sugar
¾ cup milk, or a little more
1 egg
1 cup grated American or Cheddar cheese
2 cups flour sifted with
3 teaspoons baking-powder
Dash of salt

Cream shortening and sugar. Beat the egg and add with the cheese. Mix well. Then add the flour, baking-powder and salt alternately with the milk to the first mixture. Turn into a greased, 5-by-9-inch loaf pan and bake in a moderate oven (350°) for about an hour, or until a straw inserted in the center comes out clean.

N.B. If the cheese is very dry, you need to add a little extra milk. The dough should come easily from the bowl, but not runny as pancake batter. Toasted, this is excellent for Sunday brunch with scrambled eggs. It makes fine sandwiches with deviled ham or crab salad filling. It keeps well, and is good to have on hand.

CRANBERRY BREAD

2 cups flour
½ teaspoon salt
1½ teaspoons baking-powder
½ teaspoon baking-soda
1 cup sugar
(Sift all together twice)

1 orange, juice and grated rind
2 tablespoons melted butter
Boiling water to make ¾ cup
1 beaten egg
1 cup chopped nutmeats
1 cup whole cranberries, slightly cooked (or canned whole
 cranberries, which need no cooking)

Add to the dry ingredients the egg, nutmeats, butter, hot water, orange juice and rind. Then add cranberries, and stir thoroughly.

Bake in a well-greased bread pan (5 by 9) in a slow oven (325°) for an hour or until bread draws away from side of the pan and a straw inserted in the center comes out clean. Store for 24 hours before cutting the bread.

N.B. This is delicious for tea, or toasted for breakfast or as sandwiches spread with cream cheese.

CHEESE SHORTBREAD

1 package snappy cheese (comes in a roll)
¼ cup butter or margarine
½ cup flour

Cream the butter or margarine with the cheese, then work in the flour with fingertips as a tool. Place in refrigerator for 2 hours (or overnight). Shape in thin rounds the size of a 50-cent piece. Bake 5 minutes on a cookie sheet in a hot oven (400°).

Serves 6.

HERB-BUTTERED BREAD

1 long loaf Italian bread
¼ lb. unsalted butter
1 clove garlic, crushed
¼ cup chopped parsley
¼ teaspoon oregano
Salt, pepper, paprika to taste

Cut the loaf down in wide slices almost to the bottom crust, using a sharp knife. Blend the remaining ingredients smoothly and spread the slices with the mixture. Wrap the loaf in aluminum foil and bake in a moderate oven (350°) for 10 minutes. Then pull the top foil open and leave a few minutes more for browning.

SPOON BREAD

1 pint fresh milk
½ pint white cornmeal, sifted with 1 teaspoon salt and
   ½ teaspoon baking powder
2 eggs
Butter or margarine (about half a stick), melted

Bring milk to a boil, then stir in the sifted meal, and cook until it forms a medium-thick mush. Break in the eggs, add the butter or margarine and beat well. Turn into a greased casserole (1 quart size) and bake in a hot oven (400°) about 20 minutes or until it puffs up and is delicately brown.

Serve immediately, before it falls!

Serves 4-6.

N.B. When I first had spoon bread in Virginia, I did not know whether to put it on my butter plate or on the dinner plate. I felt it might be a vegetable dish, and on the other hand, might not. There are many versions of this, but the one we use at Stillmeadow never fails to please.

For the benefit of Northerners like me, I will say you spoon it onto your plate, drop a dab of butter on it, and eat it with a fork. It is one of the best Southern dishes.

Serve it with sausage, broiled tomatoes, a green salad. Or with chicken or pork or ham. Try a left-over spoonful for a bedtime snack.

TOASTED LOAF

1 loaf unsliced bread, preferably day-old
Butter or margarine
Garlic salt or ½ clove crushed garlic

Remove the top from the loaf of bread and carefully scoop out the center, leaving ½-inch shell all around. (Use left over bread for stuffing, crumbs, or whatever.) Mix butter or margarine and garlic, and spread over the inside of the loaf. Bake in a slow oven (300°) until the loaf is crisp and delicately brown but not hard.

FILL CENTER WITH:

Hot sautéed lobster pieces, fried shrimp, or chicken.
Serve with a bowl of sauce to spoon over. For the sauce use a curry sauce, a Newburg sauce, a rich cream sauce, according to what fits the filling best. Or use canned cream of mushroom or chicken soup, diluted with half a can of milk, and heated.

N.B. It is preferable to serve the sauce separately to spoon over, so it does not soak into the casing. With a green tossed salad, this makes a meal. Add hot black coffee and a fruit compote for dessert.

For a buffet party, make several loaves and fill with different ingredients. Arrange the loaves on a large ovenproof platter and keep hot until you serve. For most fillings, a dish of grated Parmesan cheese to sprinkle over is a help.

BLUEBERRY PANCAKES

½ cup blueberries, frozen, fresh or canned, drained
1 cup milk
1 egg
1 cup pancake mix
1 tablespoon melted shortening

If you have a blender, pour everything in it but the berries, and blend. If you have no blender, shake the ingredients in a covered glass jar. The batter should be smooth. Pour about 2 tablespoons of batter at a time on a hot greased griddle. When the pancakes begin to develop bubbles, sprinkle each one with blueberries, and then turn once to finish cooking.

Serves 3-4. Use your own judgment as to how far 8 pancakes will go, when savory with blueberries, and with freshly grated maple sugar melting on them.

N.B. We favor frozen ready-to-cook baby sausages with these.

SMILEY BURNETTE'S BUTTERMILK PANCAKES

2 cups flour
2 cups buttermilk
1 teaspoon soda
1 teaspoon baking-powder
1 tablespoon sugar
½ teaspoon salt
1 egg

Mix in a blender, or beat well with a rotary beater. If it seems too thick, add more buttermilk until it is of pouring consistency. Some buttermilk is heavier, and this batter should not be stiff.

Pour into a narrow-topped bottle such as a milk bottle and let stand overnight in the refrigerator. In the morning, shake up well, and pour on a hot griddle.

If you use an ordinary griddle grease it well. If you use an electric frying pan, melt a little butter in it first.

Cook the pancakes until the edges are lacy, turn and cook just until the underside is full of bubbles.

Serve with maple sugar, honey butter, or powdered sugar.
Serves 6.

HOT-WATER PASTRY

1½ cups cake flour
½ cup shortening, preferably lard
¼ cup boiling water
½ teaspoon baking-powder
½ teaspoon salt

Place the shortening in a bowl and pour the boiling water over it. Beat until the mixture is creamy.

Sift the flour, salt, baking-powder together, and combine with the liquid ingredients, mixing well. The dough should form a soft ball. Place in the refrigerator, covered, and chill until firm.

Makes a two-crust 8-inch pie.

N.B. If you have a pastry cloth, roll out on that. Or roll between two layers of waxed paper.

Desserts

DESSERTS CAN BE the dieter's downfall. On the other hand, sometimes a small portion of a rich dessert does something for the ego. After a long stretch of cottage cheese and fruit and broiled lean chops, a Baked Apple Jubilee can restore your faith in the goodness of life.

Mama's apple pies were delicious. She used plenty of sugar and cinnamon (no nutmeg) and the crust was flaky and brown. When the pie came from the oven she made a small slit in the top crust and slipped in a spoonful of heavy cream. And it was heavy cream, a spoon could stand in it.

But in those days nobody worried about calorie counts. They had second helpings. Nowadays, we tend toward a light dessert or none at all. Cheese and crackers and a bowl of fruit make a good end to a hearty dinner. But the cheese must be good cheese whether it be a Port Salut or a nut-sweet Swiss or a robust Cheddar. The crackers must be crisp, preferably hot. The fruit should be cool but not chilled. I think it loses its flavor if it is cold.

Process cheese has many uses, but this is not one of them. For dessert-eating, only natural cheese is fitting. We serve it on a cheese board and let guests cut their own.

BAKED APPLES JUBILEE

6 large baking apples, peeled and cored
1 cup mincemeat
½ cup brown sugar (a little more if the apples are tart)
1½ cups dry white wine
1 teaspoon granulated sugar to each apple
3 teaspoons brandy or rum
1 lump of sugar
2 tablespoons brandy

Fill the centers of the apples with mincemeat and arrange them in a baking dish. Spread the brown sugar over. Pour 1 cup wine in the pan, and bake in a moderate oven (350°) until the apples are tender. Put the apples in a warm serving dish. Add the rest of the mincemeat and wine to the juices in the pan and cook 5 minutes, then pour over the apples. Sprinkle the granulated sugar and ½ teaspoon brandy on each apple. Then put the lump of sugar in a ladle, add the 2 tablespoons brandy warmed, ignite and pour it burning over the apples.

You may pass a bowl of plain thick cream if you like.

Serves 6 elegantly.

N.B. If you are not fond of brandy or rum, this is still a good dessert. And now that mincemeat comes in cans, you can make this dessert easily.

CHOCOLATE CARAMEL ICE-CREAM SAUCE

Two 1¾-ounce milk chocolate bars
¼ cup milk
14 caramels
2 teaspoons vanilla
Pinch of salt

Melt the chocolate in the milk in the top of a double boiler over boiling water, stirring until smooth.

Remove wrappers from the caramels and add. Stir again until sauce is smooth. Remove from heat and add the vanilla and salt. Cool.

Serve with ice-cream.

N.B. Could scarcely have more calories but keep the rest of the meal low in them!

CHOCOLATE CREAM

½ cup semi-sweet chocolate bits
8 marshmallows, cut in pieces (or use the new tiny ones)
½ cup heavy cream, whipped
¼ cup water
⅔ cup heavy cream

Cook the first four ingredients over low heat in a saucepan until chocolate and marshmallows melt. Remove from heat and chill. When thoroughly chilled, whip remaining cream and fold in. Freeze in ice tray in refrigerator.

Makes 1 quart.

N.B. You may use evaporated milk instead of the cream. To whip evaporated milk, chill in ice tray in freezing compartment until the edges begin to stiffen. Put milk in a cold bowl and beat with a rotary beater which you have chilled in the refrigerator.

Whipped evaporated milk may be substituted for cream in most recipes and makes a smooth, satisfactory and inexpensive substitute.

CHOCOLATE FONDUE

2 squares unsweetened cooking chocolate
1 cup soft bread crumbs
1 cup milk
1 tablespoon butter or margarine
½ cup sugar
Salt
3 eggs, separated

In a double boiler, over hot water, melt the chocolate. Add the milk and heat, stirring until blended. Then add butter, sugar, a little salt.

Beat the egg yolks lightly and stir in 2 tablespoons of the hot milk, then add them to the rest of the milk mixture. Then add bread crumbs. Let it cool until lukewarm. Meanwhile beat the egg whites until they form in peaks when you hold the beater up. Fold into the cooked mixture.

Turn into a greased baking dish (1½ quart size) or into greased individual custard cups. Bake in a moderate oven (350°) until the soufflé begins to draw away from the sides of the dish, and is delicately puffed on top. This takes from 30 to 40 minutes.

Serve hot with whipped cream.

Serves 4.

N.B. *The already-prepared crumbs are not soft enough for this dessert. Cut the crusts from freshly sliced bread, and break the centers up with your fingers, crumbling until fine. Pack firmly into the cup to measure.*

HILDA'S CHOCOLATE UPSIDE-DOWN PUDDING

1 square unsweetened chocolate
2 tablespoons butter or margarine
¾ cup white sugar
1¼ cups cake flour, sifted
2 teaspoons baking-powder
¼ teaspoon salt
½ cup milk
1 teaspoon vanilla
½ cup nutmeats, chopped

Melt the butter and chocolate together; mix with milk and vanilla. Sift dry ingredients together. Stir the chocolate mixture into the dry ingredients, add nuts and stir. Pour into a well-greased casserole.

TOPPING:

½ cup white sugar
½ cup brown sugar
2 tablespoons cocoa
1 cup boiling water

Mix dry ingredients together, and cover the pudding. Pour the boiling water over all. Bake in a moderate oven (350°) until a straw inserted comes out clean. This will take about an hour.

Serve topped with whipped cream.
Serves 4-6.

CREAM PUFFS WITH COFFEE FILLING AND CARAMEL SAUCE

¼ cup butter or margarine
½ cup water
½ cup flour with a pinch of salt added
2 unbeaten eggs

Put the butter or margarine in a pan, add the water, and bring to a boil. Then add flour. Keep heat medium high. Now take a spoon, a large one, preferably wooden, and beat the mixture as hard as you can until it comes away from the sides of the pan and makes a ball. Take saucepan from heat. Add 1 egg and beat mixture until smooth. Add the second egg and beat hard again.

Now drop the dough from a tablespoon onto a greased baking sheet, leaving several inches between each puff. Bake in a hot oven (400°) for 20 minutes. Reduce heat to medium (350°) and bake 25 minutes more. Cool.

Slit one side or cut off the top of each puff and fill with coffee cream.

Serve with caramel sauce.

Makes 8 puffs.

COFFEE CREAM:

1 cup heavy cream, whipped stiff
1½ teaspoons instant coffee
2 tablespoons sugar
¼ teaspoon vanilla

Sprinkle coffee on cream, add remaining ingredients, and beat until stiff.

CARAMEL SAUCE:

28 caramels
½ cup water

Place caramels and water in the top of a double boiler and cook over boiling water until caramels are smooth. Stir occasionally. Cool.

FLOATING ISLAND PUDDING

1 quart milk
3 egg yolks, well beaten
2 tablespoons cornstarch
2 tablespoons milk
1 cup sugar
Dash of salt
1 teaspoon vanilla
3 egg whites
¼ cup sugar

Scald the milk in the top of a double boiler. Stir in the egg yolks and add the cornstarch dissolved in the 2 tablespoons of milk. Then add the sugar and salt. Cook in the double boiler, stirring constantly until it thickens; add vanilla, and pour into a bowl.

Beat the egg whites until stiff but not dry and then gradually add the ¼ cup sugar, folding it in. Add vanilla and turn the meringue into a mould greased and dusted with sugar. Place the mould in a deep pan in 2 inches of hot water, cover, and bake in a very slow oven (250°) for 20 minutes, or until it is firm.

Cool, unmould in the center of a serving dish, and surround it with the custard. Or leave the custard in the bowl and top with the island.

Serves 4-6.

SOUR-CREAM GINGERBREAD

    1 egg, beaten
    1 cup maple syrup
    1 cup sour cream
    2⅓ cups flour, sifted with
    1 teaspoon baking-soda, and
    1½ teaspoons powdered ginger
    4 tablespoons butter or margarine, melted

Blend the egg, maple syrup and cream. Add to the dry ingredients, beating until smooth. Then add the butter or margarine and beat again. Pour the batter into a square or rectangular baking pan (8 by 10½) lined with aluminum foil or waxed paper.

Bake in a moderate oven (350°) for about 30 minutes, or until it begins to draw away from the pan.

Serve plain or frosted or with cream.

Serves 6.

HERMAN SMITH'S GINGER MOULD

1 cup milk
2 egg yolks
½ cup sugar
1 tablespoon gelatin dissolved in
¼ cup cold water
¼ cup preserved ginger, cut fine
3 tablespoons ginger syrup
1 teaspoon grated orange rind
1 teaspoon vanilla
½ pint cream, whipped stiff

Beat egg yolks slightly, add to sugar and milk with a pinch of salt. Put in a double boiler and cook over boiling water, stirring constantly. When it is thick as a custard mixture, add dissolved gelatin. Cool. Then add vanilla, ginger, syrup, orange rind. Fold in whipped cream. Chill in a mould.

Unmould and serve with sprigs of fresh mint and slices of crystallized ginger.

Serves 4-6.

N.B. Once, when Herman Smith and I were trading recipes, I admitted desserts were my downfall. This is one of my favorites, and the only difficult thing is to get preserved ginger. The crystallized is sold in most drugstores.

KING'S ARMS GREEN-GAGE PLUM ICE-CREAM

1 pint preserved green-gage plums
Juice of 2 lemons
2 cups sugar
1½ quarts milk
1 quart of cream
Dash of salt

Skin and seed and mash the plums, add the lemon juice,
sugar, milk, cream and salt, and mix well.

Freeze. If you have a home ice-cream freezer, freeze the
ice-cream in it. If not, turn your refrigerator to fast freeze.
Put the ice-cream in the ice trays and freeze. When partially
frozen, remove, and stir well to break up the crystals. Or use
a French whip. Put back in the freezing unit and freeze until
firm.

Serves 6.

*N.B. This is the best I ever ate. I begged the recipe from
John Egan at the King's Arms in Williamsburg after a dinner
that made dessert seem impossible. What with the chicken,
the rosy Virginia ham, the cornsticks, the creamed celery with
pecans, I had no wish for ice-cream. I ate a whole huge serving!*

LEMON BISQUE

3 tablespoons lemon juice
Grated rind of 1 lemon
1 can evaporated milk
1 package lemon gelatin
1¼ cups boiling water
⅓ cup honey
⅛ teaspoon salt
2 cups rolled vanilla-wafer crumbs

Put gelatin, honey, lemon juice, rind and salt into the boiling water. Let stand until slightly congealed. Then beat evaporated milk and add gelatin mixture. Put half the crumbs in the bottom of a pan (14 x 8), add the gelatin mix, top with the rest of the crumbs.

Set in refrigerator to chill well.

Cut in squares for serving.

Serves 4-6.

N.B. Evaporated milk must be thoroughly chilled in order to beat well.

This is a delicious dessert, or may be served at teatime. Because of its delicate flavor, it is perfect after a heavy dinner. Fewer calories than cake, and so easy to make.

LEMON SOUFFLÉ

4 eggs, separated
½ cup honey
½ tablespoon grated lemon rind
2 tablespoons lemon juice
Dash salt
¼ teaspoon cream of tartar

Beat egg yolks until thick and then add honey, lemon rind and juice, and continue to beat until mixture about doubles in bulk.

In a separate bowl, beat the egg whites with the cream of tartar, then fold into the yolk mixture.

Turn into a greased two-quart casserole. Set the casserole in a pan of hot water and bake in a moderate oven (350°) about 45 minutes. When it is done, the center is firm to the touch of a finger.

Serve plain or with boiled custard.
Serves 4-5.

N.B. This is not hard to make. Just be sure to do the folding gently so the whites will not lose the air. And be sure the oven is not hot.

MELON SUPREME

1 ripe canteloupe
Sauterne, or any dry white table wine

Cut out a hole in one end of the melon and scoop the seeds out with an iced-tea spoon. Pour 1 cup of wine (as needed, according to the size of the melon) in the hole. Replace the plug. Chill 4 hours in the refrigerator. Cut in wedges to serve. Garnish with mint sprigs dipped in powdered sugar.

N.B. You may arrange the wedges in a circle and fill the center with white grapes or other fresh fruit.

MERINGUES

3 egg whites
Pinch of salt
⅛ teaspoon cream of tartar
¾ cup sugar

Put a layer of aluminum foil on your cookie sheets (you need 2) and grease it, then dust with flour. Beat the egg whites until frothy, add the salt and cream of tartar and beat until the mixture is stiff enough to form a peak.

Add the sugar gradually, beating as you add. When the meringue is stiff and begins to look shiny, spoon onto the foil with a tablespoon.

Meanwhile have the oven pre-heating to 225°, or very slow. Slide the meringues gently in the oven and bake 35 minutes, but don't peek. You may then open the oven door and if they are firm and turning beige-colored, they are done. If not, leave them a few minutes more.

Cool them, after removing from foil.

Makes about 16 meringues.

Serve with fresh crushed strawberries, raspberries, or ice-cream in the centers.

N.B. An electric beater is a great help, but even without it, once you make meringues, you will use them often. You may make them ahead of time, and store them in an air-tight container.

OZARK PUDDING

¾ cup sugar
1 egg
2 tablespoons flour
1½ teaspoons baking-powder
⅛ teaspoon salt
1 teaspoon vanilla
½ cup chopped tart apples
½ cup chopped nuts

Beat egg, add sugar and beat 5 minutes with rotary beater or in a mixer.

Sift dry ingredients and add to the egg mixture. Then add vanilla, apples and nuts.

Turn into a greased pie plate and bake in a moderate oven (350°) for about 35 minutes.

Serve with whipped, sweetened cream.

Serves 4.

LEMON CHEESE SHERBET

Two 3-ounce packages of cream cheese
2 cups milk
½ cup light corn syrup
⅓ cup lemon juice
1 teaspoon grated lemon rind
2 well-beaten eggs
Few drops yellow vegetable coloring

Soften the cheese with the back of a spoon. Blend in the milk, syrup, lemon juice, grated rind and eggs. Add tint.

Pour into freezing tray of your refrigerator, and set indicator to coldest position. When almost frozen, scrape into a chilled bowl. Beat quickly with a rotary beater.

Return to refrigerator tray and freeze until firm.

Makes about 1 quart.

PINEAPPLE UPSIDE-DOWN CAKE

½ cup butter or margarine
1½ cups soft brown sugar
7 slices canned pineapple
½ cup shelled pecan halves
3 eggs
1⅓ cups white sugar
½ cup water
1 teaspoon vanilla
1½ cups flour
1½ teaspoons baking-powder
7 maraschino or candied cherries

Melt the butter or margarine and brown sugar in a heavy large frying pan (iron if possible). Lay the pineapple slices in gently. Fill the spaces with the pecans. Remove from stove and let cool.

Beat the eggs well, add the white sugar and beat 5 minutes. Then add the water and beat 5 minutes. Add vanilla. Sift the flour and baking-powder and fold into the egg mixture. Pour the batter lightly on top of the pineapple. Bake in a moderate (325°) oven about 30 minutes (or until the sponge begins to draw away from the sides of the frying pan and the top is light brown).

Carefully invert the pan on a round platter or chop plate. Fill the holes in the pineapple slices with the cherries. You may top with whipped cream.

N.B. An electric beater makes this very easy, but when I first made it, nobody had ever heard of an electric beater. I used a single, shaky hand beater. This is the best upside-down cake I ever found.

ALICE ADAMS' TEA CAKE

¾ cup sugar
½ cup butter or margarine
1½ cups flour
1½ teaspoons baking-powder
½ teaspoon salt
2 teaspoons cinnamon
½ cup milk
1 beaten egg

Mix together the sugar, butter or margarine, flour sifted with salt, and baking-powder and cinnamon. Reserve ⅓ cup for topping.

Add the milk to the egg, then add the first mixture and beat until smooth. Pour into a greased 8-inch cake pan and sprinkle the reserved topping over.

Bake 20 minutes in a moderate oven (350°) or until a straw comes out clean when inserted in the center. Serve hot.

Serves 6—but 3 can eat it all.

N.B. This is a quick and wonderful addition to tea when guests drop in, better than cake or cookies, in my opinion.

TOMATO-SOUP CAKE

1 package spice-cake mix
1 can (10½ oz.) tomato soup
¼ cup water
1 cup chopped pecans

Mix cake as directed on the package (using the soup and water for the liquid called for). Add nuts. Bake in a greased and floured 9-inch tube cake pan. Bake as directed on the package or until cake draws away from sides of the pan.

Frost with lemon icing.

N.B. This is an old-fashioned cake made the easy modern way. For the icing you may use sifted confectioner's sugar blended with lemon juice. A little grated peel helps.

LEBKUCHEN

4 eggs, well beaten
2 cups light brown sugar
2 cups flour, sifted
1 teaspoon cinnamon
¼ teaspoon allspice
½ cup mixed candied fruits and peels (or ¼ cup each citron, cut fine, orange peel, cut fine)
1 cup coarsely chopped pecans (unsalted)

Add sugar to eggs, beating until smooth. Resift the flour with the cinnamon and allspice. Add mixed fruits and nuts to the flour, then combine with the liquid mixture. Spread the dough in a greased oblong pan (8 by 11½ approximately) so that it is ½ inch deep. Bake at 375° or a moderate oven for 20-25 minutes, or until it begins to pull away from the sides of the pan and is golden on top (test with a straw if necessary).

ICING:

Sift two cups confectioners sugar and gradually stir in 3-4 tablespoons boiling water or hot cream. Flavor with 1 teaspoon rum, vanilla, or lemon juice, fresh, frozen or canned, until right for spreading easily. This should be thin and runny, it will harden. Decorate with candied cherries, citron peel, and blanched, slivered almonds, or chopped pecans.

N.B. This keeps—unless you have children standing around, and in that case, you make three or four, and then find two empty pans. It is hard to stem the tide, especially when the icing is still warm. We serve it for Christmas breakfast and hope a few pieces will be left for afternoon coffee. This also can be made ahead and frozen, provided nobody knows in what part of the freezer you have stashed it.

DESSERTS

UPSIDE-DOWN DESSERT

9 drained canned pear halves
1 box gingerbread mix

Arrange pear halves in a greased 8″ by 8″ by 2″ pan.

Mix gingerbread batter as directed and pour over pears. Bake at 375° for 30 minutes. It is done when the cake draws away from the side of the pan.

Turn out on a warm platter and serve with whipped cream. For an extra fancy touch, add slivered nuts to the cream. And you can pop a maraschino cherry in the pear halves before pouring on the batter if you wish.

Serves 4-6.

APPLE PIE ROYALE

1 package cream cheese
½ cup butter
1 cup flour
Pinch of salt

Let cheese and butter soften, then mix together, and blend in the flour, mixing lightly with fingertips. Form in a ball and chill 30 minutes in the refrigerator. Then roll out and set aside.

FILLING:

6 tart apples sliced thin
1 cup sugar
½ teaspoon cinnamon
¼ cup white raisins
Butter the size of a walnut
Juice of ½ lemon
1 jigger brandy

Mix apples, sugar, cinnamon, raisins and butter. Pour the lemon juice and brandy over. Let stand 15 minutes. Then place in an 8-inch pie pan, fit the pastry over, prick with a fork, and bake in a medium hot oven (375°) until the pastry is brown and the apples tender (you may test with a fork).
Serves 4-5.

N.B. *This is the most elegant of apple pies, well worth the time it takes.*

HAZEL'S LIME MERINGUE PIE

1 baked pastry shell, 9-inch
1 cup sugar
¼ cup cornstarch
Pinch of salt
1½ cups boiling water
3 eggs, separated
⅓ cup fresh lime juice
Rind of 1 lime, grated

Mix sugar, cornstarch and salt and put in the top of a double boiler. Add boiling water slowly, stirring constantly, and when blended place over hot but not boiling water in the lower unit of the boiler. Cook until thick and smooth.

Meanwhile beat the egg yolks, add a little of the mixture from the double boiler, stirring constantly, then return to the double boiler and cook for 2 or 3 minutes. Remove from heat and stir in the lime juice and grated rind. Blend thoroughly. Cool slightly.

Pour into the pastry shell. Beat the egg whites and pile lightly on the top of the pie. Bake in a medium oven (325°) until the meringue begins to brown.

N.B. This is from the Hazel of Ted Key's inimitable cartoons, and Hazel ought to know what is delicious. As to whether Hazel is imaginary or not, Ted Key and I feel she is a very real person. As for the pie, Hazel writes, "You never had such eatin'! ! Wahoo!"

EMMA GOLDMAN'S STRAWBERRY GLAZE PIE

1 pastry shell for a 9-inch pie, baked
2 packages frozen strawberries, thawed
⅓ cup granulated sugar
3 tablespoons cornstarch
1¼ cups strawberry juice
Custard (see below)

Strain the berries. Make the custard and pour into the pie shell when partly cooled.

Meanwhile make the glaze, as follows. Mix sugar, cornstarch and juice and cook over low heat, stirring constantly, until thick and smooth.

Lay the berries over the custard, then pour the glaze over. Chill in refrigerator. Before serving, top with whipped cream.

CUSTARD:

3 egg yolks
⅓ cup sugar
¼ teaspoon salt
2½ tablespoons cornstarch
1 tablespoon butter
2 cups scalded milk

Beat egg yolks, then gradually beat in sugar, salt, cornstarch, butter. Pour the milk over. Cook over boiling water in a double boiler, stirring until thick and smooth. Cool. Use half of this for the pie, reserve the rest for another day.

Serves 5.

N.B. It could not be richer, or more delicious. Serve it after a mixed grill (no potatoes, please) with coffee, extra black.

HOLIDAY RUM PIE

15-20 graham crackers
¼ lb. butter
⅓ (scant) cup sugar

Roll the crackers until they are fine, melt the butter, and add butter and sugar to the crumbs. Work together with fingertips until it holds together. Line a pie tin (8-inch) with this, pressing down firmly.

FILLING:

4 small packages cream cheese
½ cup sugar
2 large eggs
1 tablespoon rum

Beat the eggs, add the sugar. Add the rum to the cream cheese and, if the cheese is very stiff, a teaspoonful of cream. Combine the two mixtures and beat until creamy. Pour into the crust and bake in a medium oven (350°) for 25 minutes.

TOPPING:

1 cup commercial sour cream
3 tablespoons sugar
1 tablespoon rum

Mix well together and spread on top of the pie. Return to the oven a few minutes to heat the cream.

Serves 4-5.

N.B. *This is a fine dessert for a winter buffet. Good with country ham, broccoli soufflé, a green salad, coffee.*

What's in Your Kitchen?

YOU MAY HAVE a modern electric or gas kitchen with all the conveniences, even an ice cube breaker. Or you may have a stove, a table, and a cupboard. But you need utensils no matter what your kitchen itself may be. If there is any type I have not tried during the years, I can't think what it would be.

And my philosophy of cooking is this: choose a few utensils and do not clutter up your storage space and your working area, no matter what. At one time, when I turned my kitchen out, it was evident that 18 mixing bowls were too many. I had 9 or 10 casseroles and I always used the same 2, except for company, when I used a third.

My advice is to go through your kitchen and toss or give away any utensil you have not used in 6 months. Stillmeadow has a small kitchen (it was the milk room in 1700) but I had five cartons of utensils to discard once I saw the light.

Every cook must make her own choice. I gave away a drawerful of knives, spoons, can openers, jar openers, and such. I found, when I gave it thought, that I use: A good French paring knife (not stainless steel but one that can be sharpened on a hone). A sharp slicer and boning knife. A serrated knife for slicing tomatoes and bread. A fat, heavy knife for opening squash and such. A clam knife. Two paring knives. A grapefruit knife. A potato peeler. A gadget that nips a lemon peel off.

I use: one long-handled 2-tined fork. One small 4-tined fork.

I use: two wooden spoons, one long-handled, one short. One slotted spoon. Two large metal spoons. One set of measuring spoons. One spatula. One pancake turner. One French whisk. One rotary beater.

I use: one chopper. One pastry blender. One flour sifter. One potato masher. One juice can opener. One bar-tool (opens bottles or jars, pries tops from containers). One rolling pin.

A good wall can opener, and a wall opener for screw-topped jars are essential.

I have several measuring cups in different sizes, but I seldom use any but the 1-cup or 2-cup size, and could settle for 1.

I use two strainers, one small, one large, and one set of graters. I have a meat grinder but seldom use it because I hate to clean it. I chop in my wooden bowl or use the electric blender. The electric mixer is important, for it doubles as a juicer. Also the two bowls can be used for many things.

Since I reduced my stock of mixing bowls, I find I need only three: one large, one medium, one small.

I use three casseroles, small, medium, large. For a big party, I use the large glass baking dish for such things as Lasagna, macaroni and cheese or whatever. I use one small rectangular glass baking dish at practically every meal. I have two glass baking dishes (round) that have covers which may be used separately.

I have two pressure cookers, one very large (16-qt. size), one the 3-quart size. A Dutch oven is a must, and a loaf pan for bread or meat loaf, 4½" x 8½".

I use two skillets, one small, with a cover, one iron,

large size. But the electric frying pan is my standby. This also doubles for stews, small pot roasts, and a dozen other things. (Smiley Burnette makes cakes in his, but I can't manage it.) I use a steamer big enough for sweet corn or small lobsters; and the middle piece doubles as an extra strainer.

I use two glass pie plates (which double for casseroles), two baking sheets, two layer cake pans, one square loaf pan.

I choose a glass double boiler. For saucepans, I actually use only three although I have six.

A coffeemaker, tea kettle, and toaster pretty well complete the list of what I need to cook with.

I like individual ramekins and custard cups, and my egg poacher. And my cast iron popover tins are a help.

An electric waffle iron is handy.

We pop corn in the electric frying pan.

Actually this amount of equipment fits into a small kitchen and still leaves room to turn around. A few extras such as the chafing dish, the casserole candle-warmer, the French earthenware casserole and such, I store in the back kitchen with the big turkey platter, the scallop shells, and most of the cookie cutters. I keep just one cutter in the cutlery drawer, for cookies and canapés.

When I had my eighteen mixing bowls, seven would be used, one at a time, and stacked in the sink. But with three, I rinse each one out, and use it again. I find two paring knives do the job of ten if I take two seconds to clean them between onions and apples.

And an uncluttered kitchen is so much more restful to work in, and so much easier to keep clean!

Shelf Magic

THE FIRST TIME a carload of unexpected guests turned up at Stillmeadow, I was desperate. I did not know then that this always happens when you have completely used up everything in the refrigerator, because you want to defrost it. You have divided up the last of the pot roast and the last of the creamed chicken among the cockers and the Irish setter. You gave the bread to the birds. Also that last end of cake, and three doughnuts. You planned on a boiled egg for lunch because there are not enough eggs to scramble. The egg woman comes that night.

My worst experience was the day Jon Whitcomb came to discuss the illustrations for a book of mine. He was due around four but came around noon, because he got away early. And of course he had had no lunch. (Nobody ever arrives at Stillmeadow having eaten.) He came in, gay, charming, handsome—and hungry! He had lunch, but we said we had already eaten. That half-broiler just could not serve three. By five o'clock, I began to have dizzy spells.

This really inaugurated a planning program for me, so it was a worthwhile experience. Jill whitewashed the area at the top of the cellar stairs and built four stout shelves. (It is better to have your emergency shelves OUTSIDE your regular kitchen, because it is easier to check on the supplies, also you don't sneak them out when you don't need them.)

On the top shelf we put spices, mustards, Worcestershire sauce, pepper, salt and so on. (Have you ever run

239

completely out of salt?) Also on this shelf go instant coffee, cocoa and powdered milk.

The second shelf is reserved for packaged mixes, spaghetti, macaroni, noodles, rice, dehydrated soups and gravies.

The third shelf we use for two cans each of our favorite canned soups and vegetables (including canned onions and canned potatoes). Also we store canned mushrooms, canned beef and mushroom gravies.

The fourth shelf contains two cans each of different types of fish, two jars of chicken, one can beef tongue. And also meal-in-one cans, such as beef stew, corned-beef hash, spaghetti and meatballs, canned whole chicken, canned ham. And one can each of our favorite canned fruit.

The shelf magic does not interfere with the deep freeze. But it means we can serve dinner in a few minutes, without even unwrapping a package and allowing longer cooking times so the food can thaw. The emergency shelves take little care. No defrosting. We simply check off what we use on a pad in the kitchen and the next time we shop, we buy replacements.

There is practically no limit to the good meals you can prepare with mixes and cans. For instance, canned beef stew takes a dash of burgundy, and is topped with parsley dumplings made from a biscuit mix. Baked beans go in a large greased casserole, and I bury a small onion in the center, cut through into eighths. I add dry mustard, a little brown sugar, more salt and pepper, and lay a couple of slices of partially cooked bacon on top. I bake until bubbly.

And dinner is served!

Herbs, Seasonings, Spices

COOKING WITH HERBS is a fine art. But you do not have to use all the herbs there are when you start the rewarding adventure. Buy small containers, for herbs lose their freshness after long storage. If you grow your own, harvest them as they begin to flower, wash well, and dry in a dark cool room.

Here is my basic list.

BAY LEAVES, a must for topping meat loaves, and in soups, stews.

BASIL, for tomato dishes, in beef stew, and when cooking shellfish.

DILL, for salads, dressings, sauces.

MARJORAM, roast beef, lamb, or veal, and in egg and fish dishes.

MINT, sauce for lamb, with boiled potatoes, with tea.

OREGANO, in spaghetti sauce, potato salad, in fish butter for shellfish.

PARSLEY, salads, dressings, soups, stews.

ROSEMARY, in chicken, pea, spinach soup, in stuffings, in scrambled eggs.

SAFFRON, in rice dishes, Arroz con Pollo (chicken), in chicken soup.

SAGE, stuffing for poultry or roast pork.

SAVORY, bean or pea soup, fish chowders, beef, boiled fish, salads.

TARRAGON, salad dressings, sauces, aspics.

THYME, lamb, chicken stuffing.

241

Herb butter is made by blending herbs and butter (preferably sweet butter). Use 1 level tablespoon of minced fresh green herbs or ½ teaspoon dried herbs to 2 oz. butter. Add a dash of lemon juice. Use on fish for broiling, with eggs, on asparagus, with broiled meats, or in sandwiches.

Garlic is in a category by itself. It is often called an herb, but it is a root vegetable as is the onion, the way I look at it. Its uses are infinite, from rubbing a cut clove on a steak to mincing it for barbecue sauces. Beside the garlic cloves, garlic powder and garlic salt are essentials.

Here is a list of my basic spices:

ALLSPICE, for soup stock, pea soup, pot roasts, boiling fish or shellfish.

CINNAMON, stick or ground for pies, toast, apple cobblers, baked pears.

CHILI, I use this lavishly in egg dishes, soups, stews, chili con carne, barbecue dishes.

CLOVES, stick in ham, add to meat stews or soups, with boiled fish, in pickled beets.

CURRY, fish dishes, with lamb, sprinkled over boiled rice, in deviled eggs.

GINGER, in fruit compotes, Bavarian-cream desserts.

MACE, in oyster stew, fish sauces, in cream sauce for vegetables.

NUTMEG, Jill won't eat it. I use cinnamon instead. Even on eggnogs and custards and in rice puddings.

My favorite single seasoning is seasoned salt, available in most stores. I use it almost always in place of regular salt, except for some desserts that call for flour sifted with dash of salt, etc. I use freshly ground pepper, wearing out a good many pepper mills in the course of a year or so, but it is worth it. I keep an assortment of mustards, the mild Dijon type, the Bahamian, regular, horseradish, dry mustard (English type) and a barbecue mustard.

I use meat tenderizer for most meats.

I use monosodium glutinate in spite of its hideous title. I keep it with my seasoned salt and pepper mill right by the range. I have not written it in many recipes in this book, simply because I hate to keep copying it down. And if I call it MSG it sounds like an automobile. It is not, strictly speaking, a seasoning, but it reinforces the flavor of whatever you are cooking.

I use wine, but that is a matter for the individual cook to settle for herself. I keep 1 bottle of dry white table wine, 1 bottle of dry burgundy, 1 bottle of dry sherry, 1 bottle of rum (a half-pint for this) and 1 bottle of brandy (for flaming plum puddings and such). Properly used, just a spoonful of wine adds a delicate flavor. There are available several booklets and one or two excellent books dealing with wine cookery, not to mention the huge *Gourmet Cookbooks* (2 volumes) which make a fine addition to the cookbook shelf.

But when all's said and done, the priceless seasoning is not to be bought in any store. Better than fillet of beef in aspic with truffles served in an unhappy silence, is the simplest casserole served with love and laughter.

Index

245

INDEX

247

INDEX

INDEX

INDEX